# The yīn House Handbook
# 陰宅手冊

setting up a tomb by way
of sān hè fēngshuǐ

by
Hung Hin Cheong

# The yīn House Handbook 陰宅手冊
## setting up a tomb the sān hè way 三合立向法

All intellectual property rights including copyright in relation to this book belong to Joey Yap Research Group Sdn. Bhd.

No part of this book may be copied, used, subsumed, or exploited in fact, field of thought or general idea, by any other authors or persons, or be stored in a retrieval system, transmitted or reproduced in any way, including but not limited to digital copying and printing in any form whatsoever worldwide without the prior agreement and written permission of the copyright owner. Permission to use the content of this book or any part thereof must be obtained from the copyright owner. For more details, please contact:

**Joey Yap Research Group Sdn. Bhd.** (944330-D)
19-3, The Boulevard, Mid Valley City,
59200 Kuala Lumpur, Malaysia.
Tel           : +603-2284 8080
Fax          : +603-2284 1218
Email      : info@masteryacademy.com
Website  : www.masteryacademy.com

Text © 2012 Hung Hin Cheong
Design and illustrations © 2012 by Joey Yap Research Group Sdn. Bhd.
All rights reserved.
First Edition June 2012
Second print July 2018

DISCLAIMER:

The author, copyright owner, and the publishers respectively have made their best efforts to produce this high quality, informative and helpful book. They have verified the technical accuracy of the information and contents of this book. However, the information contained in this book cannot replace or substitute for the services of trained professionals in any field, including, but not limited to, mental, financial, medical, psychological, or legal fields. They do not offer any professional, personal, medical, financial or legal advice and none of the information contained in the book should be confused as such advice. Any information pertaining to the events, occurrences, dates and other details relating to the person or persons, dead or alive, and to the companies have been verified to the best of their abilities based on information obtained or extracted from various websites, newspaper clippings and other public media. However, they make no representation or warranties of any kind with regard to the contents of this book and accept no liability of any kind for any losses or damages caused or alleged to be caused directly or indirectly from using the information contained herein.

# Table of Contents

| FOREWORD BY JOEY YAP | |
|---|---|
| PREFACE | |

| Part-1: The Case for Burial fēngshuǐ | 1 |
|---|---|

| Part-2: Setting up a Facing (立向) | | 7 |
|---|---|---|
| Chapter-2.1 | sān hè luó pán (三合羅盤) | 9 |
| Chapter-2.2 | Dragon Vein (以龍配向) | 13 |
| Chapter-2.3 | Water Considerations (水法) | 27 |
| Chapter-2.4 | Matching Dragon to Water (山水通氣) | 39 |
| Chapter-2.5 | Assessing the Embraces (撥砂法) | 51 |

| Part-3: Personalizing the Facing (仙命宜忌) | | 57 |
|---|---|---|
| Chapter-3.1 | Principles | 59 |
| Chapter-3.2 | Compatibility Tables | 67 |
| Chapter-3.3 | Gold Divisions | 129 |
| Chapter-3.4 | Other Restrictions | 137 |
| Chapter-3.5 | Multiple Occupancy Tombs | 141 |
| Chapter-3.6 | Pre-selecting a Burial Plot | 145 |

| Part-4: Ancillary Features | | 149 |
|---|---|---|
| Chapter-4.1 | Water Drainage | 151 |
| Chapter-4.2 | Earth Deity | 157 |
| Chapter-4.3 | Miscellaneous | 167 |
| Chapter-4.4 | Tomb Construction | 173 |

| Part-5: Date Selection | | 179 |
|---|---|---|
| Chapter-5.1 | Why Select a Date | 181 |
| Chapter-5.2 | Personalizing a Date | 189 |
| Chapter-5.3 | Some Practical Issues | 195 |

| End Note | 203 |
|---|---|
| Appendix-1: Chinese Characters | 205 |
| Appendix-2: Human Plate 5 Elements | 209 |
| Appendix-3: nà yīn Elements | 217 |
| About the Author | 241 |

# Foreword by Joey Yap

Over the years, Mr. Hung Hin Cheong has never failed to inspire me in his many relentless quests to perfect his scholastic endeavor in Chinese Metaphysical studies. His enthusiasm and contributions towards the field of Feng Shui have benefited many students and enthusiasts alike. His past project includes unveiling the secrets of classical Xuan Kong Feng Shui through his comprehensive commentary and transliteration of the Four Celebrated Poems of Xuan Kong. Besting his previous effort yet again, with this new book, I believe he has laid a concrete foundation for the practice, knowledge and application of one of the most important, albeit sadly underrated aspect of Feng Shui - the Yin House Feng Shui.

The book you have in front of you holds significant importance as it is the first of its kind in the world to be published in English. This book is integral because most practitioners today do not know how to apply and benefit from the application of Yin House Feng Shui, as it is not included as a standard syllabus in many of today's modern mainstream classes. Never before has anybody in the English speaking world attempted to branch out and deliver a comprehensive look at Yin House Feng Shui study.

When Mr. Hung presented me with the idea of publishing this book, I hesitated a little because I realized the lack of written material on this field was due to the very, very niche market associated with the subject matter. Secondly, it's such a complicated subject and even in our live classes, it was never easy to teach. Quite frankly, I wasn't confident that this topic would be a popular subject for the general public to obtain a copy of this book. Fortunately, as fervent a scholar as he is a lover for Classical Feng Shui, Mr. Hung is not motivated by commercial mass market interest and he convinced me to give this book a chance. Already a successful businessman in his own term, Mr. Hung have invested considerable time out of his busy schedule to meticulously research and compile all the information needed to make this book a reality. When I read the final manuscript, I have to say, I am very pleased with his work and I know, this would make teaching Yin House Feng Shui so much easier and I am sure, all our Academy's student would love it. This book is truly a labour of love, written for the genuine enthusiasts and students of Feng Shui.

Essentially, Yin House Feng Shui is the original form of Feng Shui. This fact has widely misunderstood and eluded by many, including countless popular Feng Shui enthusiasts themselves. In its most vital definition, Yin House Feng Shui pertains to the study of the places for the dead. Yin House Feng Shui has its origins way back during the Qin Dynasty. However, many classics written on Yin House Feng Shui were penned during the renaissance era of the Tang Dynasty.

In fact, Yin House Feng Shui was a deeply rooted component of the Tang Dynasty, and it was used recurrently to select the burial spot for many deceased Emperors. The interests in Yin House Feng Shui took a backseat when the practice and principles of Feng Shui extended, as the field progressed and advanced, to another discipline: Yang House Feng Shui, the study of places for the living during the Ming and Qing Dynasty.

Despite the heavily important values and histories associated with this field, Yin House Feng Shui is often mistaken by the modern society as a "taboo" or "bad omen", and irrevocably neglected or overlooked by many in their quests to become an established Feng Shui practitioner. And it is another common misconception that, in order to practice Yin House Feng Shui, one needs to be well-versed in spiritual prayers or mantras, in order to protect him or herself from the bad omen that entails from the ritual. In reality, there is absolutely nothing eerie or spiritual about Yin House Feng Shui as it doesn't promote elaborate rituals, supernatural intervention or superstitious practices. Contrary to all this, you will discover from reading this book, that Yin House Feng Shui is a systematic, formula based science of harnessing the Qi from the land. In fact, one of my teachers told me when I first learnt Yin House Feng Shui is that it brings a lot of good karma to the practitioner because Yin House Feng Shui (when applied correctly) can bring positive effects to an entire family spanning a few generations whereas Yang House Feng Shui can only affect the residents of a house and for a limited time frame.

In layman's terms, Yin House Feng Shui is often regarded as the Feng Shui Trust Fund for the next generations. When one embarks on practicing and applying the Yin House Feng Shui approach, he or she is laying the concrete foundation of wealth, luck and longevity in a neat "saving fund" for his or her children and grandchildren. It is from the Yin House that we can ascertain how long the prosperity will be with a person's family and the number of generations that will enjoy the prosperity.

If you're a careful observer, you'll notice that balance in Feng Shui cannot be achieved without the presence of the Yin and the Yang. When an ancestor is buried in a place with favorable Feng Shui, the next generations or descendants of his will get to reap the benefits of Yin House Feng Shui, and at the same time, relish as their Yang House Feng Shui becomes strengthened and more powerful. This illustrates the importance of balance in Feng Shui practice. In order to exercise Yin House Feng Shui, one needs to begin his or her education early as it is a more complex system, with four elaborate stages and requires a higher level of commitment as compared to Yang House Feng Shui. The four stages include landform identification, selection of meridian spot, burial and tomb alignment. In this book, Mr. Hung generously shares with his readers the techniques of Burial and Tomb Alignment. Yin House Feng Shui, even at its very basic understanding, is a vast subject, even more elaborate and detailed than its Yang House counterpart. There are various schools, techniques and methods to practice, understand and to perfect this elusive art. Mr. Hung's book focuses on the San He system's perspective.

In reality, anyone with the heart and spirit to become an inspiring Feng Shui Master must someday graduate to learning Yin House Feng Shui. This is such a profound subject, and it is in no way possible to be separated from the core of Classical Feng Shui learning. Almost all the principles we observe in Yang House Feng Shui today stemmed from their original sources in Yin House techniques.

Having said all that, I must applaud Mr. Hung for his efforts and enthusiasm in creating this book, which is a must read for all Feng Shui enthusiasts and inspiring Feng Shui Masters everywhere.

If you're thinking of deepening your understanding on this matter, you have here the perfect handbook to kick start your own unbounded journey to Yin House Feng Shui application. It doesn't matter whether you're in it for your own understanding or for the application in your life, Yin House Feng Shui is an interesting subject to dwell upon, and it should be deservedly appreciated by Feng Shui aficionados everywhere!

Warmest regards,

Joey Yap
Founder of the Mastery Academy of Chinese Metaphysics
June 2012

www.joeyyap.com | @DatoJoeyYap

# Preface

The book started off as a set of notes – a sort of aide memoir – to help with my yīn house (tomb) consulting work. Gradually the contents expanded, drawing from different sources and augmented by field experience. So I decided to compile the notes into a book which I hope will help to guide the novice practitioner embarking on yīn house work, and also become handy reference material for seasoned practitioners.

There are 2 general approaches to yīn house fēngshuǐ: sān yuán (三元) which is time dependent; and sān hè (三合) which is much more enduring. Personally I favour the sān hè approach, as tombs by their very nature are permanent structures. Most people would not want to relocate their forebears' tombs if they can help it.

The handbook is intended to be a practical tool. It will focus on practical instructions, and dispense with theoretical discussions, but be assured that each step of the way is founded solidly on classical sān hè fēngshuǐ principles. Neither is it just text book material. Some of the traditional practices are no longer relevant in modern times, and need to be re-interpreted according to present-day realities.

The fēngshuǐ master's primary tool is the classical compass called a luó pán (羅盤). It comes in several forms. The form we shall be using is the sān hè luó pán. The reader is expected to know how to operate this instrument.

The reader is also expected to know, by heart, the Chinese characters for the 10 "Heavenly Stems" 甲乙丙丁戊己庚辛壬癸; 12 "Earthly Branches" 子丑寅卯辰巳午未申酉戌亥; and 8 "Trigrams" 乾兌離震巽坎艮坤. Their Romanized pīnyīn versions will not be quoted. Readers who wish to be reminded of these 30 characters should turn to Appendix-1.

The other Chinese annotations that appear within parenthesis in the text are included for reference only. They are not critical for understanding the main body of information.

Classical fēngshuǐ may be broadly divided into 2 disciplines: "Landforms (巒頭)" and "qì Management (理氣)". The 2 disciplines work hand-in-hand: landforms identify a site with high potential; qì management then steps in to set up the tomb to extract maximum benefit from the site. One without the other is incomplete. The techniques described herein fall under qì management.

Landforms must be learnt elsewhere. In fact there is no short cut to learning landform fēngshuǐ other than to trek the mountains and observe the landforms first hand, under the guidance of an experienced master. This is a task way beyond the scope of any handbook.

Part-1 of the book is a short exposé on the linkage between burial and its postulated effects on the deceased person's descendants. Whereas in traditional Chinese culture, this link is accepted as an article of faith, our modern supposedly rational society often demands an explanation, and rightly so. A rational hypothesis is put forward. The topic of cremation versus burial is also explored.

Part-2 discusses the setting up the tomb's facing direction (立向). This is the key step in yīn house fēngshuǐ after a favourable plot has been identified based on landforms. 3 factors will be discussed: "Dragon", water and Embraces. These jargon terms will be explained in due course.

Part-3 deals with personalizing the tomb facing to the deceased person's innate compatibilities based on his birth year. In practice, this evaluation should even precede plot selection as the best plot, landform wise, cannot be put to good use if the plot orientation is incompatible with the occupant. Here again, traditional practice imposed a multitude of taboos that needed to be reassessed and selectively trimmed to fit in with modern realities. These days there are relatively few designated burial grounds, and tomb orientations are often severely restricted by the demarcated plot boundaries and rules imposed by the cemetery management.

Part-4 looks at some ancillary features commonly found in Chinese tombs, in particular, water drainage of the tomb enclosure, and the Earth Deity. Tomb construction is mentioned but only briefly. The outward appearance of a tomb is largely cosmetic, governed more by cultural and social factors than by fēngshuǐ.

Part-5 addresses date selection for burial. There are many ways to select a date. The "Gods & Killings (神煞)" method is introduced but not discussed in detail. It would take much more than a handbook like this to cover the topic of date selection adequately. The selected date has to be personalized for the deceased. The sān hè method of date personalization is described in order to be consistent with the sān hè fēngshuǐ techniques used to align the tomb.

Part-5 also discusses some of the practical limitations and issues that the modern practitioner has to deal with. Theory and traditions notwithstanding, it is practicality that rules the day.

The Appendices are a treasure trove of information. Appendix-2 discusses the "Human Plate 5 Elements" and Appendix-3 "nà yīn Elements". To the best of my knowledge, no other English book has hitherto explored these topics to any depth.

To students of fēngshuǐ, burials should never be regarded as a morbid topic. It is a much needed service to the bereaved family at a time when the family needs help. Fēngshuǐ practitioners are first and foremost service providers. If we shirk from our duties, not only do we dishonour our profession, we should really be asking ourselves "What are we here for?"

The techniques described herein are my preferences. Every master is entitled to his favourite techniques. The ultimate objective of gathering and tapping into the qì is common, but the chosen paths may be different. As the saying goes, "Each and every highway leads to Rome."

Master Joey Yap has graciously consented to write a Foreword for this book. Master Joey has opened the door to classical fēngshuǐ for me and encouraged me to research the classics. For this I am deeply indebted.

*from the ramblings of one hhc, a fengshui crazee*
**May - 2012**

# Part-1

## The Case for Burial fēngshuǐ

## Part-1: The Case for Burial fēngshuǐ

To Westerners and Western trained minds, the Chinese tradition of honouring their ancestors is often called "ancestor worship". This is a much misarraigned term. The Chinese do not worship their ancestors as deities or supernatural beings. They honour their ancestors first for giving life to the family lineage, and secondly they believe there is a linkage between the generations that transcends death. They take the view that events past present and future are inexorably linked in a universal web, and births and deaths are but minor blips in this greater network. [Think Internet!]

Is that a religion? Is Carl Jung's concept of synchronicity a religion? I wouldn't have thought so. But what about the candles and joss sticks and other paraphernalia normally associated with prayer? That's just ceremony, a show. The same could be done with flowers or a eulogy if preferred. Just as effective, or just as irrelevant, depending on how one looks at it.

As human beings live and die on this earth, it stands to reason that there exists a connection between the energy of the earth and human life. This all pervasive energy is called "qì (氣)". The quality of this qì varies depending on the locality, and human life is affected by this qì in several ways.

During a person's lifetime, his wellbeing is affected, not entirely but to a very significant extent, by the environment in which he lives. Fēngshuǐ principles are applied to optimize the qì at his place of abode. That is called yáng house fēngshuǐ. The qì that originates from the earth, in a manner of speaking, rubs off on the person and becomes "human qì", although in absolute terms it is the same qì.

When that person dies, the qì that is associated with him does not vanish just like that. After all, qì is a form of energy, and even modern science recognizes that energy cannot be created or destroyed, merely transformed from one state to another.

# Part-1: The Case for Burial fēngshuǐ

It is postulated that if the person's remains are interred, i.e. returned to the earth, a transformation takes place. The qì that was associated with the person transforms into a "signal", for want of a better word, that can be picked up by other persons who share a common bloodline with him, irrespective of their geographical locations. [Think radio waves that propagate across geographic boundaries.] "DNA signature" is a modern term that the ancients did not know about, but the idea was the same.

If the burial is done at a location rich in positive qì (生氣), the signals generated will be wholesome and will impact the lives of the recipients positively. Conversely, if the remains are interred at a location without positive qì, or worse still, with negative shā qì (煞氣), then the signals generated will be corrupted and the descendents picking up the corrupted signals will have their lives screwed up.

The practice of finding burial locations having positive qì, and orientating the tomb to optimize receipt of this qì, is called yīn house fēngshuǐ.

The above is of course only a hypothesis. I don't think it will ever be proven conclusively one way or the other, not until scientists perfected time travel, forward and back.

In the old days, dedicated fēngshuǐ masters claimed to have studied numerous old tombs and researched the fortunes of the affected families several generations down the line. Astonishing correlations were claimed, but we do not know how impartially these researches were done.

For now, we have to be satisfied with a hypothesis. The Chinese, past and present, are a practical people. The claimed benefits may or may not accrue, but what's there to lose? As long as one can afford the cost of the burial plot and the services of a good fēngshuǐ master, why not give it the benefit of the doubt?

## Part-1: The Case for Burial fēngshuǐ

In modern times, cremation has become more commonplace. It is convenient and less messy. The question is how would cremation affect the link between an ancestor and his descendants?

In fact cremation is nothing new. Buddhist monks through the ages have been cremated. Although it was pointed out that these monks did not have descendants and therefore nobody to pass on to, we ought to take a broader view. Many of the senior monks were eminent scholars and philosophers, and their teachings that transcended many generations were in a way their descendants. These monks were cremated and their ashes interred in stupas or pagodas. Visits to ancient monasteries revealed that fēngshuǐ principles were observed in the location of these stupas.

It was also on record that the Qīng Dynasty emperor, Shùn Zhì (順治, 1638-1661), was cremated and his ashes interred in a tomb that had superlative fēngshuǐ. The Qīng Dynasty continued to prosper after him, and survived for another 250 years.

Hence a conclusion may be drawn that provided the ashes are interred properly after cremation, the linkage mechanism described earlier continues to operate. Indeed modern burial grounds do offer mini plots for urn burial.

Another question commonly asked is about placement of urns in a multi-tiered columbarium. Would this constitute proper burial?

This question is similar to condo living compared with landed property. Technically, it is preferable for the urn to be in contact with the earth, just as a landed property will respond to fēngshuǐ treatment better than a condo. But also like modern living, many people, by necessity or by choice, live in a high rise condo.

## Part-1: The Case for Burial fēngshuǐ

In cases where the columbaria are built into the hillside, as some of them are, then there is not much difference between these and landed plots. Other columbaria are free standing units under roof, sometimes several stories high. In such cases the connection to earth is somewhat tenuous. One view is that such a burial will have minimal effect on the people aspect (progeny) of later generations, but it will impact the wealth aspects if the niche facing is selected properly.

What about lodging of urns at temples? As this practice has a religious dimension, I choose not to discuss it here.

Then there is the practice of scattering the ashes into the sea or river. From the fēngshuǐ perspective, this is undesirable as it will mean a severance of the connection between the generations. The later generations will not be able to inherit the qì of their ancestors. Of course it can be argued that no connection is preferred to a flawed connection, but let us not be drawn into that argument. It takes us nowhere.

Instead let us move on to the steps we need to take in order to tap into the available qì at a selected location. This will be covered in Parts-2, 3, 4 and 5 that follow.

# Part-2

## Setting up a Facing

# CHAPTER-2.1
## sān hè luó pán (三合羅盤)

Part-2: Setting up a Facing (立向)

# CHAPTER-2.1
## sān hè luó pán (三合羅盤)

As we are applying sān hè fēngshuǐ in this book, we shall be using the sān hè luó pán. A professional sān hè luó pán has close to 30 rings. Of these, the most important are the 3 layers of "24-Mountains" rings. They are named "Earth Plate", "Human Plate" and "Heaven Plate" respectively.

Before launching into the main body of discussions, let us briefly reacquaint ourselves with these 3 rings, which will be referred to repeatedly in Part-2 of this book. See Fig-1.

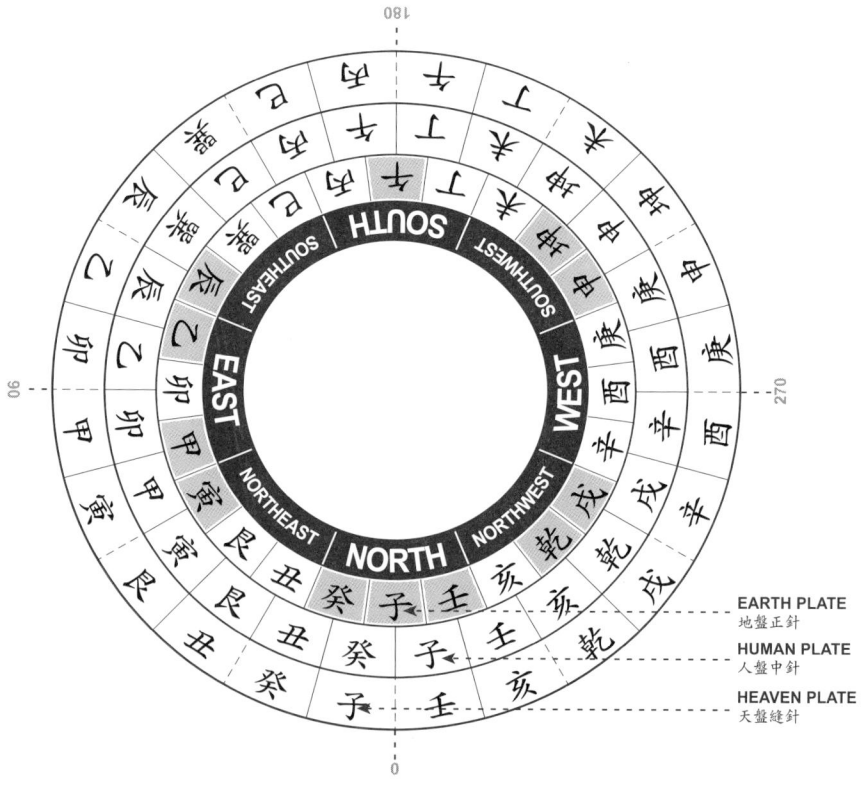

**Fig-1: sān hè luó pán**

# Part-2: Setting up a Facing (立向)

Take note that the polarities yīn (black characters on white background) and yáng (black characters on coloured background) are determined by the Earth Plate alone.

Also note that the Mountains on the Heaven Plate are paired: 壬子, 癸丑, 艮寅, 甲卯, 乙辰, 巽巳, 丙午, 丁未, 坤申, 庚酉, 辛戌, 乾亥.

The Earth Plate is used for measuring the "Dragon" and facing, and the Heaven Plate is used exclusively for water measurements. The Human Plate is used to measure Embraces.

A firm grasp of the luó pán fundamentals will help to avoid confusion later.

# CHAPTER-2.2
## Dragon Vein

Part-2: Setting up a Facing (立向)

## CHAPTER-2.2
## Dragon Vein (以龍配向)

1. This chapter deals with the earth qì entering the tomb. This qì originates from faraway mountains, but only emperors in the old days had the resources to trace the qì path way back to its ultimate source.

For lesser mortals, and certainly for us in this age of quick fixes, it is enough to assess the last leg of the qì path just before it enters the tomb. In classical fēngshuǐ terminology, this is the "Dragon Vein (龍脈)" that feeds qì into the tomb.

In other words, we only need to measure the final Dragon Vein entering the tomb, and the multiple rises and falls of the Dragon further back may be ignored (千里來龍但看到頭八尺).

Strictly speaking, identifying Dragon Veins is a landform skill that has to be learnt, but this too has been simplified. We stand at the prospective plot and look for a rise in the land, or mound, usually at the back or to one side of the plot. The high point of that rise is deemed to be the top of a Dragon Vein running down to the plot.

Measure the top of the Vein from the plot, using the 24-Mountains Earth Plate (Fig-1 inner ring). That gives us the required Dragon Vein direction[1].

---

[1] This is only a "deemed" Dragon Vein. Strict sān hè theory defines Veins quite differently. Our modern interpretation relies on the principle that earth qì travels down a hill slope starting from the highest point of that slope.

The method works most of the time as burial plots are usually located on hill slopes facing downhill, but there are exceptions. Sometimes the Vein is much harder to pinpoint, and there are even cases where there is no discernible Vein at all.

# Part-2: Setting up a Facing (立向)

In common usage, this Dragon Vein is loosely called "Incoming Dragon (入首龍), or simply "Dragon"[2].

2. Next, determine the yīn or yáng polarity of the "Dragon" according to the Earth Plate of the sān hè luó pán (Fig-1 inner ring). The facing (向) of the tomb must be of the same polarity as the "Dragon". This is a fundamental requirement[3]. See Fig-2.

---

[2] Strictly speaking, "Incoming Dragon" is a misnomer here. The real "Incoming Dragon" in sān hè fēngshuǐ is not measured from the tomb but from the "Gap Crossing" behind the "Main Mountain", but we do not need to bother with these technicalities in our present discussions. Just be mindful that when we say "Dragon" in this context, we are in fact referring to the Vein that enters the tomb.

Readers who have studied sān hè fēngshuǐ will know that technically the Vein should be measured using the "60 Earth Penetrating Dragons (透地六十龍)" plate. However this plate is difficult to use in practice. The method prescribed herein is much more user friendly even if somewhat diluted.

[3] Please note the point of reference is the face of the tombstone, and that when the facing is of one polarity, yīn or yáng, the sitting need not be of the same polarity. It is the facing that matters in this formula.

# Part-2: Setting up a Facing (立向)

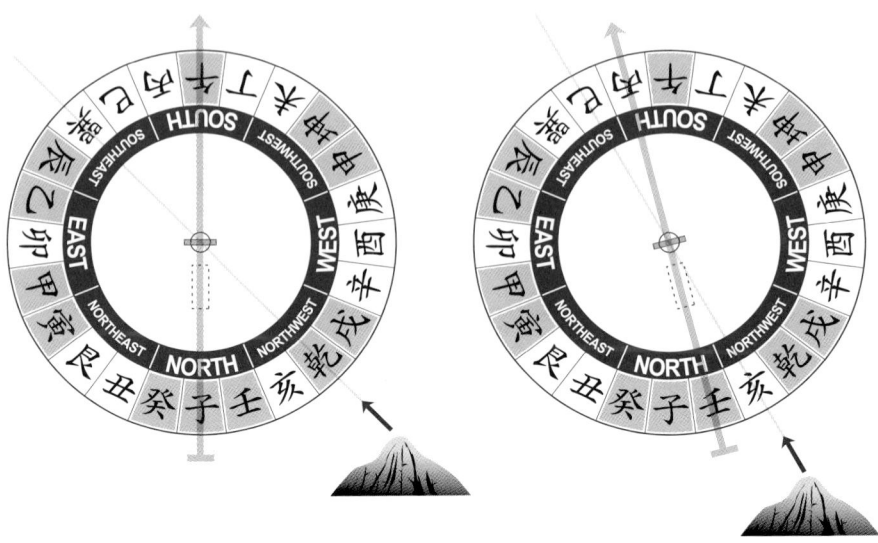

乾 (yáng) Dragon 午 (yáng) facing - compliant

亥 (yīn) Dragon 丙 (yīn) facing - compliant

乾 (yáng) Dragon 丙 (yīn) facing - non-compliant

**Fig-2: Pure yīn pure yáng 淨陰淨陽**

Part-2: Setting up a Facing (立向)

3. There are 6 standard criteria for establishing a facing based on the "Dragon":

   a. "Pure yīn pure yáng (淨陰淨陽)" i.e. yīn "Dragon" yīn facing, yáng "Dragon" yáng facing, according to the sān hé 24-Mountains plate, as follows:

| yáng | yīn |
|---|---|
| 乾 | 艮 |
| 甲 | 丙 |
| 坤 | 兌(酉) |
| 乙 | 丁 |
| 離(午) | 巳 |
| 壬 | 丑 |
| 寅 | 震(卯) |
| 戌 | 庚 |
| 坎(子) | 亥 |
| 癸 | 未 |
| 申 | 巽 |
| 辰 | 辛 |

The yīn House Handbook

## Part-2: Setting up a Facing (立向)

b. "bā guà pair-bonding (八卦正配)" i.e. select a complementary guà pair according to the Early Heaven bā guà and their nà jiǎ (納甲) derivatives:

| "Dragon" | facing |
|---|---|
| 乾, 甲 | 坤, 乙 |
| 艮, 丙 | 兌, 丁, 巳, 丑 |
| 震, 庚, 亥, 未 | 巽, 辛 |
| 離, 壬, 寅, 戌 | 坎, 癸, 申, 辰 |

Also applies vice-versa, i.e. 坤, 乙 "Dragon" - 乾, 甲 facing, etc.

c. "Within each nà jiǎ group (納甲一氣)" i.e.

| "Dragon" | facing |
|---|---|
| 乾, 甲 | 乾, 甲 |
| 坤, 乙 | 坤, 乙 |
| 艮, 丙 | 艮, 丙 |
| 兌(酉), 丁, 巳, 丑 | 兌(酉), 丁, 巳, 丑 |
| 震(卯), 庚, 亥, 未 | 震(卯), 庚, 亥, 未 |
| 巽, 辛 | 巽, 辛 |
| 離(午), 壬, 寅, 戌 | 離(午), 壬, 寅, 戌 |
| 坎(子), 癸, 申, 辰 | 坎(子), 癸, 申, 辰 |

# Part-2: Setting up a Facing (立向)

d. "3 harmonies (三合局)" i.e. a "Dragon" may be paired with a facing if the 2 belong to the same 3-harmonies group:

艮丙辛，寅午戌
坤壬乙，申子辰
巽庚癸，巳酉丑
乾甲丁，亥卯未

provided the selected pair has the same yīn-yáng polarity, and there is a further recommendation that a Branch "Dragon" should not be paired with a Branch facing for fear of the energies becoming too strong during certain years.

A Branch "Dragon" should therefore be paired with a Stem facing, or vice versa; or a Stem "Dragon" with another Stem facing.

e. "Heavenly Nobles (天乙貴人)" i.e. based on the Heavenly Nobles song, certain "Dragons" can be matched with certain facings, provided they are of the same yīn-yáng polarity, as follows:

| "Dragon" | facing |
|---|---|
| 丙，丁 | 亥，酉 |
| 庚 | 丑，未 |
| 乙 | 申，子 |

Also applies vice-versa, i.e. 亥，酉 "Dragon" - 丙，丁 facing, etc.

The other Stems and Branches mentioned in the song contravene the uni-polarity rule and are unusable.

Part-2: Setting up a Facing (立向)

f. "Early/Later Heaven (先/後天)" i.e. the Trigram to which the facing belongs and the Trigram to which the "Dragon" belongs, bear an Early/Later Heaven Trigram relationship between them. For example, Trigram 乾 is the Later Heaven equivalent of Trigram 離. So a 乾 facing, and by extension also a 甲 facing, is related to a 離 (午) "Dragon", and by extension also a 壬 or 寅 or 戌 "Dragon".

The Early/Later Heaven relationships of the 8 Trigrams are listed below:

| Early Heaven | Reference Trigram | Later Heaven |
|---|---|---|
| 離 | 乾 | 艮 |
| 巽 | 兌 | 坎 |
| 震 | 離 | 乾 |
| 艮 | 震 | 離 |
| 坤 | 巽 | 兌 |
| 兌 | 坎 | 坤 |
| 乾 | 艮 | 震 |
| 坎 | 坤 | 巽 |

# Part-2: Setting up a Facing (立向)

4. In establishing a facing, the "8-Killing Forces" formula must never be violated, as follows:

   坎 (壬子癸) "Dragons", tomb must not face 辰 or 戌
   坤 (未坤申) "Dragons", tomb must not face 卯
   震 (甲卯乙) "Dragons", tomb must not face 申
   巽 (辰巽巳) "Dragons", tomb must not face 酉
   乾 (戌乾亥) "Dragons", tomb must not face 午
   兌 (庚酉辛) "Dragons", tomb must not face 巳
   艮 (丑艮寅) "Dragons", tomb must not face 寅
   離 (丙午丁) "Dragons", tomb must not face 亥

   The reverse also holds true, i.e. a 辰 or 戌 "Dragon" should not be paired with a 子 (坎) facing, etc. The adjacent Stem facings (壬 and 癸 in this instance) are allowed as Stems have a milder effect.

5. A Branch facing (立地支向) will receive stronger qì, both positive and negative, than a Stem facing (立干維向). The effects will also be more durable, but it does mean that during certain years when the "Grand Duke (太歲)" or "3-Killings (三煞)" visit that Branch, the affected Branch facing is more vulnerable.

   A Stem facing is milder.

# Part-2: Setting up a Facing (立向)

6. Then there is the principle of oblique qì entry. That is to say, qì coming down the "Dragon" should enter the tomb at an angle, and not directly from behind. [There are ways to get around this. See paragraph 7.]

The technical term is "qì entry through the ear or waist" (腰耳乘氣)".

What constitutes "ear entry" or "waist entry"?

If the angle between the tomb axis and the "Dragon" axis is not more than 4 Mountains (60°) on the luó pán, it is considered "ear entry". Anything more than that is "waist entry". qì entering through the ear is preferred as it produces quicker effects.

What we want to avoid is the "Dragon" qì penetrating the head end of the casket. Such a situation is detrimental, and is described as "receiving head-on qì busts the brains" (直來直受，氣衝腦散).

In fact, oblique qì entry is already in place as long as the top of the "Dragon Vein" is not directly behind the tomb. The only variances are ear or waist entry, and left or right side.

Both left and right entries are acceptable. In practice the local landscape usually dictates that. For example, if the top of the Vein is somewhere on the left hand side as one looks up from the tomb (facing uphill), then the qì will be entering through the right ear or right waist.

Fig-3 illustrates this principle.

# Part-2: Setting up a Facing (立向)

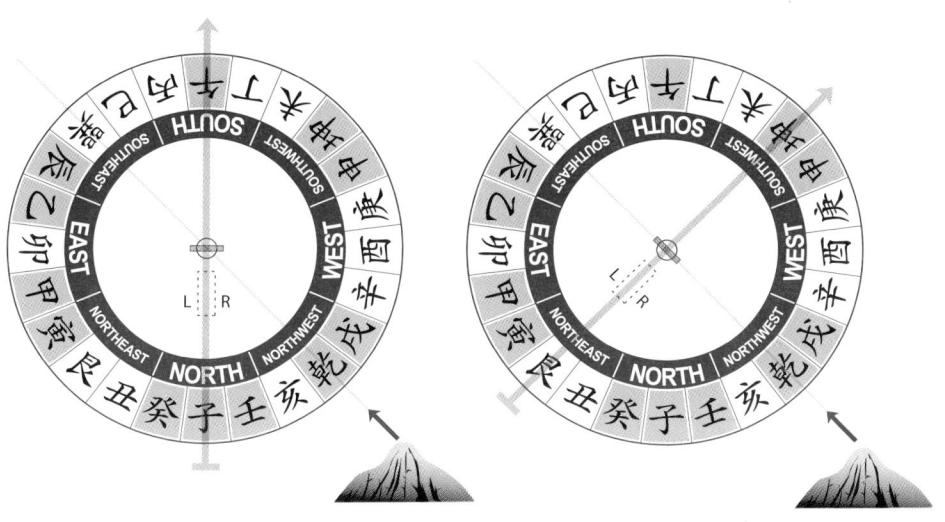

**qì entry through the right ear**  **qì enters through right waist**

**Tilt casket to avoid qì crashing through the crown (para 7)**

**FIG-3: qì entry through the ear or waist**

# Part-2: Setting up a Facing (立向)

7. Sometimes there are other compelling factors that require a tomb facing to be directly in line with the "Dragon". For example, the "Dragon" enters from 亥, and site conditions disallow a major tilt of the tomb. We then end up with a 亥 "Dragon" and a tomb sitting 亥 facing 巳. The "Dragon" qì enters the tomb directly from behind.

   In such a case, the casket should be laid at an angle to the tomb facing in order to avoid the problem of "receiving head-on qì busts the brains" (para 6 above). A few degrees tilt is enough. Just get the casket axis away from the "Dragon" axis.

   Do remember that the tomb facing is determined by the tombstone facing, not the axis of the casket. In the above example, the tomb facing remains at 巳 even if the casket is tilted away to the 壬-丙 axis.

   [*Reminder:* all measurements of "Dragon" and facing are taken using the 24-Mountains Earth Plate.]

8. Apart from the "Dragon", water and Embraces (消砂納水) are also key considerations in selecting a tomb facing.[4]

   Chapter-2.3 discusses the water requirements, and Chapter-2.4 matches "Dragon" to water. Embraces will be discussed in Chapter-2.5

---

4 The early fēngshuǐ schools took the "Dragon" to be the primary criterion for selecting a facing, but there were detractors. Other masters (as early as the Sòng Dynasty) argued that water should take precedence instead.

# CHAPTER-2.3
## Water Considerations (水法)

Part-2: Setting up a Facing (立向)

## CHAPTER-2.3
### Water Considerations (水法)

1. Several methods are available for assessing water formations. The method described herein is called the "Later Heaven Water Method (後天水法)".[5]

2. Whereas the "Dragon" and the facing are obtained using the 24-Mountains Earth Plate, the 24-Mountains Heaven Plate (天盤縫針) is used for water measurements (Fig-1 outer ring).

3. In the Heaven Plate, the 24 Mountains are grouped into 12 "Paired-mountains" (雙山) as follows: 壬子, 癸丑, 艮寅, 甲卯, 乙辰, 巽巳, 丙午, 丁未, 坤申, 庚酉, 辛戌, 乾亥.

4. The "Later Heaven Water Method" operates on the concept of the "12-Growth Phases (十二長生)". There are altogether 8 sets of the phases, each set being applicable to a type of qì defined by its element (Wood, Fire, Metal or Water)[6] and its polarity (yáng or yīn).

    The 12 phases are:
    "Growth (長生)"; "Bath (沐浴)"; "Youth (冠帶)";
    "Officer (臨官)"; "Prosperous (帝旺)"; "Weakening (衰)";
    "Sickness (病)"; "Death (死)"; "Grave (墓)";
    "Extinct (絕)"; "Conceive (胎)"; "Nurture (養)",
    in sequential order.

---

[5] Of course this is not the only water method in sān hè fēngshuǐ. Some schools use other methods like "Earth Principles 5 Verses (地理五訣)" and "4 Major Water Structures (四大水局)", but I found the "Later Heaven Water Method" to be more user friendly.

[6] The astute reader will have noticed that the element Earth is missing. In fact, Earth is incorporated into Water in this application, but we do not need to be bothered with the underlying theory for now.

## Part-2: Setting up a Facing (立向)

In our present discussions, only the "Growth", "Prosperous", "Weakening" and "Grave" phases are significant. These are listed in the following table for each type of qì:

|  | Growth | Prosperous | Weakening | Grave |
|---|---|---|---|---|
| 甲 yáng Wood qì | 乾亥 | 甲卯 | 乙辰 | 丁未 |
| 乙 yīn Wood qì | 丙午 | 艮寅 | 癸丑 | 辛戌 |
| 丙 yáng Fire qì | 艮寅 | 丙午 | 丁未 | 辛戌 |
| 丁 yīn Fire qì | 庚酉 | 巽巳 | 乙辰 | 癸丑 |
| 庚 yáng Metal qì | 巽巳 | 庚酉 | 辛戌 | 癸丑 |
| 辛 yīn Metal qì | 壬子 | 坤申 | 丁未 | 乙辰 |
| 壬 yáng Water qì | 坤申 | 壬子 | 癸丑 | 乙辰 |
| 癸 yīn Water qì | 甲卯 | 乾亥 | 辛戌 | 丁未 |

5. Water flowing from left to right (左水倒右) (standing at the tomb looking out) is labeled yáng qì, which can be 甲 Wood, 丙 Fire, 庚 Metal or 壬 Water; and water flowing from right to left (右水倒左) is labeled yīn qì, which can be 乙 Wood, 丁 Fire, 辛 Metal or 癸 Water.

## Part-2: Setting up a Facing (立向)

6. In the application of the "Later Heaven Water Method", first determine the direction of water flow in front of the tomb: whether left to right (yáng qì), or right to left (yīn qì). Then select to face either "Prosperous" (立旺向) or "Weakening" (立衰向) according to the following table. The word "Weakening (衰)" may not sound appetizing, but it is just a name. In fact the word should be read as "beyond Prosperous (旺餘)" in the present context. Receiving "Weakening" qì is no less desirable than receiving "Prosperous" qì under the "Later Heaven Water Method".

The 24 possible facings[7] are tabulated below:

|  | Prosperous facings | Weakening facings | Type of qì |
|---|---|---|---|
| For left to right water: (yáng) | 甲卯 | 辰 | 甲 Wood qì |
|  | 丙午 | 未 | 丙 Fire qì |
|  | 庚酉 | 戌 | 庚 Metal qì |
|  | 壬子 | 丑 | 壬 Water qì |

---

7 At this juncture, I must qualify myself in that the use of the word "facing" in the present context is not strictly correct and can be misleading.

Instead of "Prosperous facing", the technically correct term should be "tomb axis penetrating Prosperous on the Heaven Plate". But that's a mouthful and too technical. So I decided to err on the side of brevity. The problem is that the words "Prosperous facing" and "Weakening facing" herein could give the false impression that facings are measured using the Heaven Plate, which is misleading.

Moreover, almost all the published material on the "Later Heaven Water Method" use these misleading terms. So for convenience I joined the crowd. Readers should be mindful that facings are always measured using the Earth Plate, and that any reference to facings in connection with the Heaven Plate is but a convenient figure of speech. More of this is discussed in Chp-2.4

## Part-2: Setting up a Facing (立向)

| | Prosperous facings | Weakening facings | Type of qì |
|---|---|---|---|
| For right to left water: (yīn) | 艮寅 | 癸 | 乙 Wood qì |
| | 巽巳 | 乙 | 丁 Fire qì |
| | 坤申 | 丁 | 辛 Metal qì |
| | 乾亥 | 辛 | 癸 Water qì |

7. Ideally water should exit[8] at the "Grave" direction, but water exits at "Sickness" or "Death" or "Extinct" are also acceptable. Alternatively water may also exit at "Weakening"[9] (except we do not want the tomb facing to be directly in line with the water exit, which could happen if the tomb faces "Weakening").

Likewise, water entering from "Growth" is ideal, but entries from "Youth" or "Officer" or "Prosperous" are also acceptable. Even "Weakening" is acceptable at a stretch. There used to be a traditional bias against water entering from "Bath", as "Bath" is associated with "Peach Blossom (桃花)" (euphemism for physical attraction). But in modern society, many careers and business/personal successes are indeed built on "Peach Blossom". So "Bath" water has become respectable somewhat.

---

8 The term "water exit" here describes the point at which the waterway leaves the visible landscape, eg. where the river disappears round a bend as observed from the front of the tomb. This "exit" is different from the "drain outlet" discussed in Chp-4.1. Likewise, the term "water entry" in this chapter refers to the point at which the waterway is seen to enter the territory within sight.

9 The "Grave" direction is called the "Principal storage (正庫)" of water, whereas the "Weakening" direction is called the "Borrowed storage (借庫)".

# Part-2: Setting up a Facing (立向)

8. There are 4 common water formations in front and to the sides of a tomb, as follows:

a. "Horizontal Water Formation (橫水城)" where the water flows across the front of the tomb in either the left to right (yáng), or right to left (yīn) direction;

b. "Oblique Water Formation (斜水城)" where the water either enters from the left rear quadrant and exits at the right front quadrant (yáng), or enters from the right rear quadrant and exits at the left front quadrant (yīn);

c. "On-coming Water Formation (逆水城)" where the water enters from directly in front and exits either at the right rear quadrant (yáng) or at the left rear quadrant (yīn);

d. "Flow Away Water Formation (順水城)" where the Water enters either from the left rear quadrant (yáng) or from the right rear quadrant (yīn), and exits directly in front of the tomb.

## Part-2: Setting up a Facing (立向)

The above water formations are illustrated in Fig-4 below:

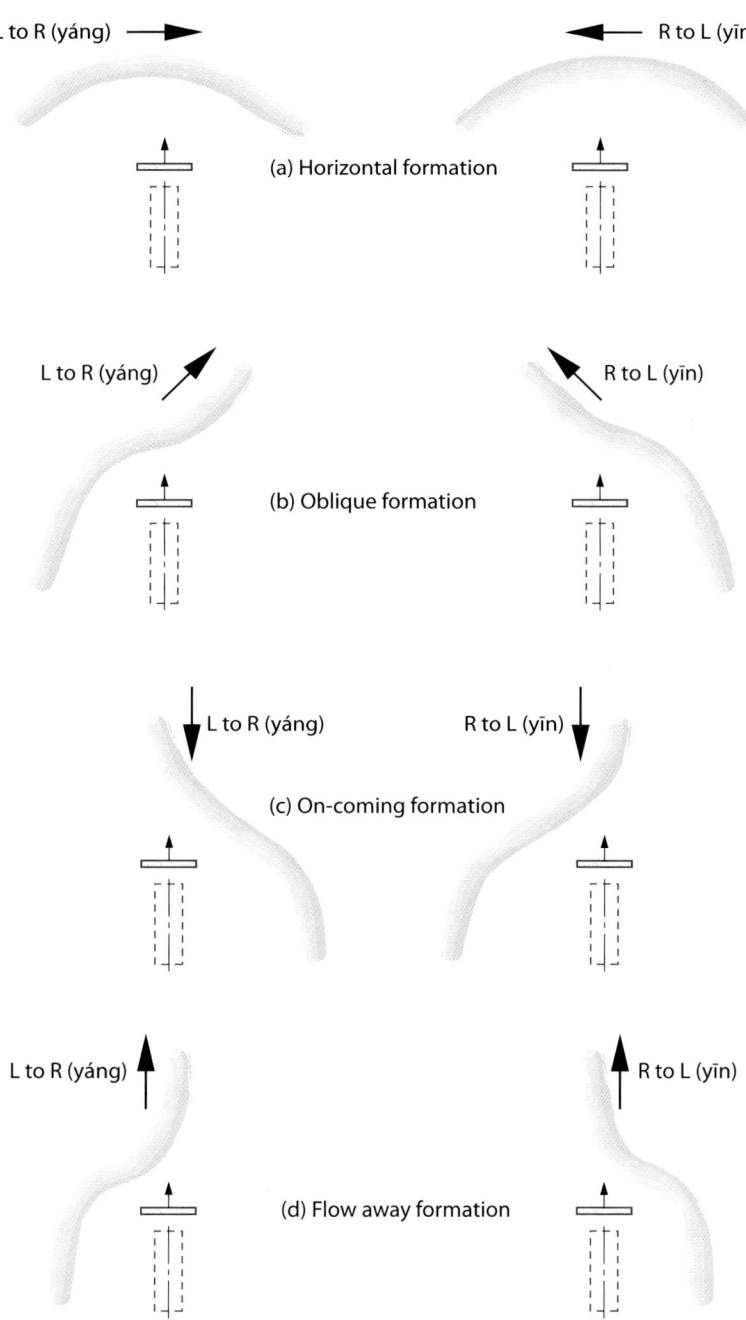

## Part-2: Setting up a Facing (立向)

In any of the water formations described above, a satisfactory facing may be found that complies with the rules set out in items 6 and 7 above, except that water exiting directly in front is risky, and one is usually better off avoiding the "Flow Away Water Formation".

Water exiting at a Stem Mountain is preferred over exiting at a Branch. Stems are pure, whereas Branches are more susceptible to shā qì at certain times.

[*Reminder:* all water measurements are taken using the 24-Mountains Heaven Plate.]

9. In establishing a facing based on water considerations, care should be exercised that the "8 Roads of Destruction" formula should not be violated, as follows:

   庚 or 丁 facing, water must not exit at 坤
   Conversely, 坤 facing, water must not exit at 庚 or 丁
   乙 or 丙 facing, water must not exit at 巽
   Conversely, 巽 facing, water must not exit at 乙 or 丙
   甲 or 癸 facing, water must not exit at 艮
   Conversely, 艮 facing, water must not exit at 甲 or 癸
   辛 or 壬 facing, water must not exit at 乾
   Conversely, 乾 facing, water must not exit at 辛 or 壬

   Only the Stem facings are affected by this formula.

## Part-2: Setting up a Facing (立向)

10. The standard approach is to first identify a suitable facing based on the "Dragon" using the Earth Plate, and then try to match this facing with the water requirements using the Heaven Plate.

    As a Mountain on the 24-Mountains Earth Plate straddles 2 Mountains on the Heaven Plate, it is sometimes possible to adjust, or tweak, the facing within the same Mountain on the Earth Plate to also satisfy the water requirements determined by the Heaven Plate. Some examples of this tweaking are described in Chp-2.4

11. A facing that meets both "Dragon" and water requirements simultaneously is naturally preferred, but if this cannot be achieved, an option exists to align the casket below ground level to meet the "Dragon" requirements, and align the tombstone differently to meet the water requirements. This practice of dual alignments was applied to many historically significant tombs.

    The facing of a tomb is invariably defined by the front face of the tombstone. In the case of dual alignments, the tomb facing is still determined by the tombstone (so-called external axis), but the casket alignment (internal axis) is usually inscribed somewhere on the tombstone for information. Both casket and tombstone alignments are measured using the Earth Plate.

## Part-2: Setting up a Facing (立向)

12. Then there may be cases where the "Dragon" is indeterminate, or a satisfactory match between "Dragon" and water is unobtainable even with dual alignments. In such an event, there is the option to set aside the "Dragon" requirements and establish a facing based solely on water considerations (舍龍就向).

    The rationale is that the "Dragon" takes a long time (generations) to manifest its effects whereas water acts much more quickly (within 6~10 years, according to some). Hence a facing derived solely from water considerations should at least be able to deliver wealth benefits to the first generation descendants.

13. What if there is no visible water in the vicinity? In that case, a valley or ravine between 2 ridges, even if dry, is treated as a channel for water flow. The flow direction would then be determined by the terrain, i.e. from high to low, from narrow to wide.

# Part-2: Setting up a Facing (立向)

**Application Notes**

In modern fēngshuǐ applications, roadways are regarded as virtual water, to be evaluated the same way as real waterways. In many modern "terraced" cemeteries, it is not uncommon to have certain stretches where the pathway in front of the burial plots slopes down in one direction, say from left to right, whereas the real water flow that follows the general terrain is in the opposite direction, say from right to left.

In such a scenario, do we opt for a yáng facing based on the pathway, or a yīn facing based on the real water flow?

There are 2 contradictory factors to consider:

a. Real water is many times more powerful than virtual water;
b. The nearer water will deliver the bigger impact.

In the present case, the real water flow is some distance away while the pathway is immediately in front of the plot.

In such a scenario, a judgment call is required. By my reckoning, if the real water flow based on the general terrain is quite far away and not visible from the plot, then it is safe to use the pathway as the reference.

On the other hand, if the real water is clearly visible, and especially if there is an expanse of water (natural or man-made lake) which would serve as a substantial qì reservoir, then the effect of the real water is likely to overwhelm that of the pathway. It would therefore be logical to base our computations on the real water flow.

There are of course marginal cases where a clear-cut decision is difficult. We can infer that such locations are undesirable as they suffer from a confused qì flow.

# CHAPTER-2.4
## Matching Dragon to Water (山水通氣)

Part-2: Setting up a Facing (立向)

## CHAPTER-2.4
### Matching Dragon to Water (山水通氣)

The objective is to select a facing that meets both the "Dragon" requirements (Chp-2.2) and the water requirements (Chp-2.3).

*Case study #1:*

The "Dragon" enters from 亥 and a 丙 facing is selected. This complies with the "Pure yīn pure yang" principle, as both 亥 and 丙 are yīn Mountains (Chp-2.2 para 3a). In addition, 亥 is a Heavenly Noble of 丙 (Chp-2.2 para 3e). Hence a 丙 facing is eminently suitable from the "Dragon" perspective.

[*Reminder:* "Dragon" and facing are measured using the Earth Plate.]

If water in front of the plot flows from left to right, ideally (but not necessarily) entering from 艮寅 ("Growth" of 丙) and exiting 辛戌 ("Grave" of 丙), we have 丙 yáng Fire qì (Chp-2.3 para 4). If the tombstone facing penetrates the Heaven Plate through the 丙午 Paired-mountains, we have achieved the desired "Prosperous" facing (Chp-2.3 para 6).

To do this, we have to tilt the tombstone slightly clockwise so that its faces the second half of 丙 Mountain on the Earth Plate (closer to 午), i.e. compass reading 165~172.5°

# Part-2: Setting up a Facing (立向)

This scenario is illustrated in Fig-5 below:

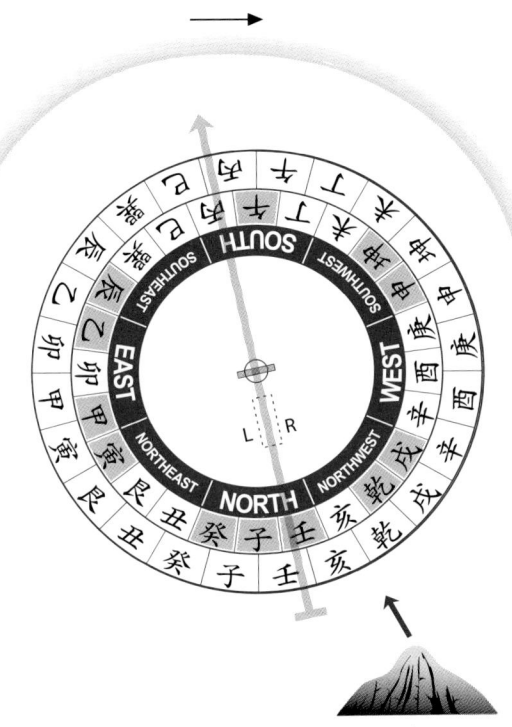

亥 "Dragon" (Earth Plate)
Tomb facing 丙 (Earth Plate)
L-R horizontal water formation
丙午 "Prosperous"
yáng Fire qì (Heaven Plate)

**FIG-5: 丙 facing, yáng "Horizontal Water Formation"**

Part-2: Setting up a Facing (立向)

*Case study #2:*

The same "Dragon" and facing as in case study #1, but the water flow is from right to left, ideally entering from 庚酉 ("Growth" of 丁) and exiting 癸丑 ("Grave" of 丁). We have 丁 yīn Fire qì (Chp-2.3 para 4). To become "Prosperous", the tombstone facing must penetrate the Heaven Plate through the 巽巳 Paired-mountains (Chp-2.3 para 6).

This is done by tilting the tombstone slightly counterclockwise so that its faces the first half of 丙 Mountain on the Earth Plate (closer to 巳), i.e. compass reading 157.5~165°

The scenario is illustrated in Fig-6 below:

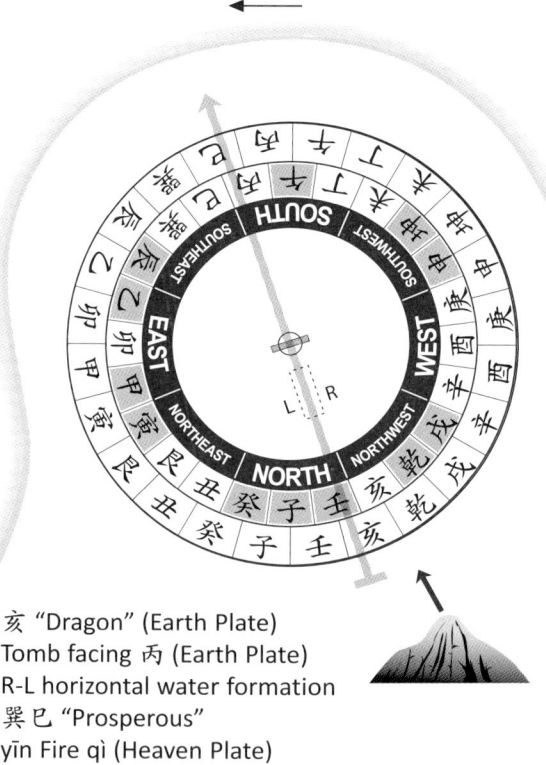

亥 "Dragon" (Earth Plate)
Tomb facing 丙 (Earth Plate)
R-L horizontal water formation
巽巳 "Prosperous"
yīn Fire qì (Heaven Plate)

**FIG-6: 丙 facing, yīn "Horizontal Water Formation"**

## Part-2: Setting up a Facing (立向)

*Case study #3:*

The "Dragon" enters from 戌 and a 甲 facing is selected. This complies with the "Pure yīn pure yáng" principle, as both 戌 and 甲 are yáng Mountains (Chp-2.2 para 3a). In addition 戌, being a nà jiǎ derivative of 離, has an Early/Later Heaven relationship with 甲 by virtue of the latter being a nà jiǎ derivative of 乾 (Chp-2.2 para 3f). This makes 甲 a very suitable facing for a 戌 "Dragon".

If the water flow is an "Oblique Water Formation" that enters from, say, 乾亥 ("Growth" of 甲) at the left rear quadrant, and exits at 乙辰 ("Weakening" of 甲) at the right front quadrant, we have 甲 yáng Wood qì (Chp-2.3 para 4). The 甲 facing (Earth Plate) penetrates 甲卯 (Heaven Plate) and hence becomes "Prosperous", if the tombstone is tilted slightly clockwise (closer to 卯) (75~82.5°). See Fig-7.

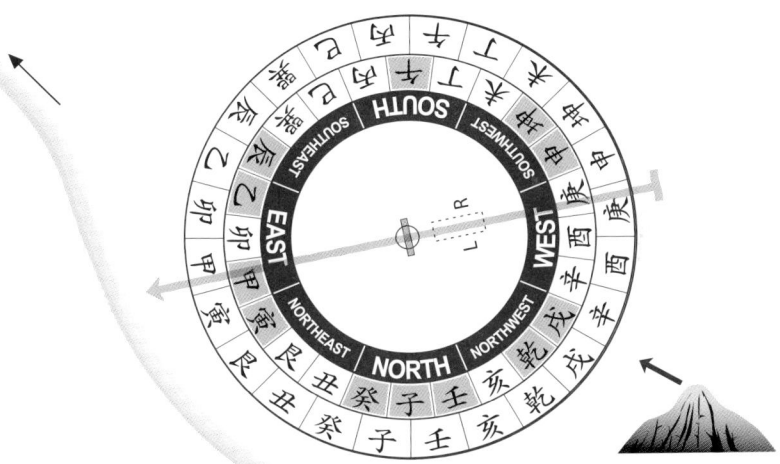

戌 "Dragon" (Earth Plate)
Tomb facing 甲 (Earth Plate)
L-R oblique water formation
甲卯 "Prosperous"
yáng Wood qì (Heaven Plate)

**FIG-7: 甲 facing, yáng "Oblique Water Formation"**

Part-2: Setting up a Facing (立向)

*Case study #4:*

Same "Dragon" and facing as in case study #3, but the water enters from 丙午 ("Growth" of 乙) at the right rear quadrant and exits at 癸丑 ("Weakening" of 乙) at the left front quadrant. This constitutes an "Oblique Water Formation" sporting 乙 yīn Wood qì (Chp-2.3 para 4).

If the tombstone facing 甲 (Earth Plate) is tilted slightly counterclockwise (closer to 寅) so that the axis penetrates 艮寅 on the Heaven Plate (67.5~75°), then the facing will attain "Prosperous" status (Part-2 para 4). See Fig-8.

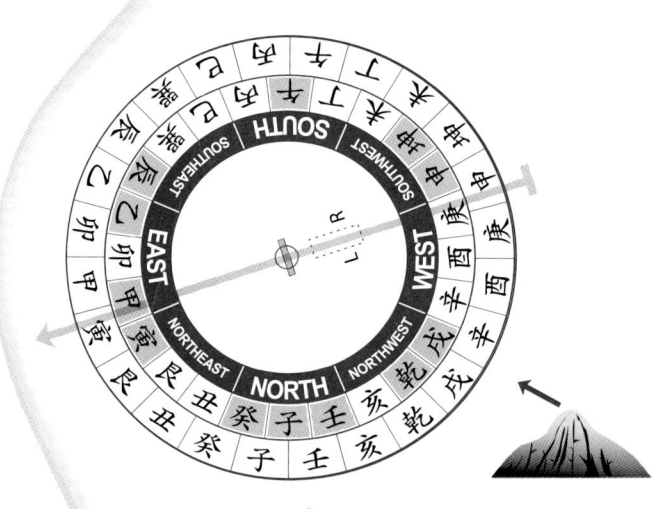

戌 "Dragon" (Earth Plate)
Tomb facing 甲 (Earth Plate)
R-L oblique water formation
艮寅 "Prosperous"
yīn Wood qì (Heaven Plate)

**FIG-8: 甲 facing, yīn "Oblique Water Formation"**

## Part-2: Setting up a Facing (立向)

*Case study #5:*

The "Dragon" enters from 坤 and a 乙 facing is selected. Apart from complying with the "Pure yīn pure yáng" principle (坤 and 乙 are both yáng), 乙 is also a nà jiǎ derivative of 坤 (Chp-2.2 para 3c). This makes 乙 a very suitable facing for a 坤 "Dragon".

The water enters from 乙辰 ("Weakening" of 丁), almost directly in front of the tomb facing, and exits at 癸丑 ("Grave" of 丁) at the left rear quadrant. This is a case of "On-coming Water Formation" bearing yīn Fire qì (Chp-2.3 para 8c).

The 乙 facing (Earth Plate) penetrates 乙辰 on the Heaven Plate, and hence receives "Weakening" qì under the "Later Heaven Water Method" (Chp-2.3 para 6). See Fig-9.

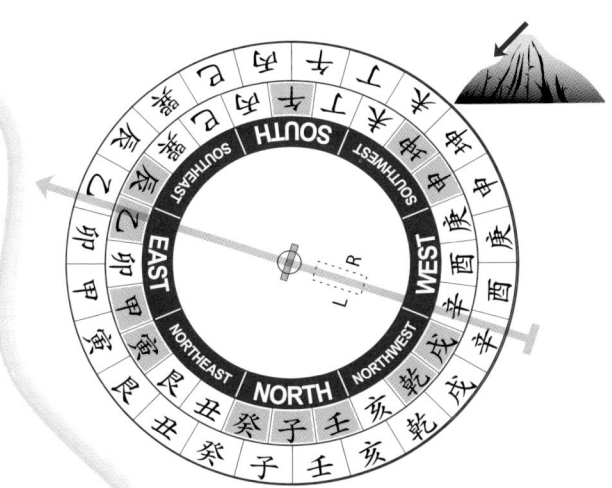

坤 "Dragon" (Earth Plate)
Tomb facing 乙 (Earth Plate)
R-L oblique water formation
乙辰 "Weakening"
yīn Fire qì (Heaven Plate)

**FIG-9:** 甲 facing, yīn "Oblique Water Formation"

## Part-2: Setting up a Facing (立向)

The above case studies are some examples of how the "Dragon" and water requirements may be met simultaneously by judiciously tweaking the tombstone facing. This manoeuvre is only effective for Stem facings, as each Stem Mountain on the Earth Plate sits astride 2 Paired-mountains on the Heaven Plate.

The same is not true of the Earth Plate Branch Mountains, as the entire Branch Mountain sits within the same Paired-mountains on the Heaven Plate.

In other words, a Stem facing (Earth Plate) is able to accommodate both left-to-right and right-to-left water, whereas a Branch facing does not have this flexibility unless it is one of the so-called "4 Graveyards" 辰/戌/丑/未. I shall leave it to the reader to figure out for himself why this is so.

Clearly, different situations require different treatments, and the ingenuity of the fēngshuǐ master is called upon to find the optimum solution in each case.

Sometimes it is just not possible, or practical, to find a facing that satisfies both "Dragon" and water requirements simultaneously. In our deliberations, do not forget the "8 Killing Forces" (Chp-2.2 para 4), and the "8 Roads of Destruction" (Chp-2.3 para 9). Sometimes a facing that looks promising may, on closer examination, turn out to violate "8K" or "8Roads". In such difficult cases, alternative measures may have to be adopted, as suggested in Chp-2.3 para 11 and 12.

# Part-2: Setting up a Facing (立向)

In fact some practitioners prefer to select facings based entirely on water considerations, the rationale being:

- Water delivers much quicker results than the "Dragon";

- On flat land, the "Dragon" is often hard to discern;

- Even when the plot is located on a slope, the deemed "Dragon" may not be real, as in a modern cemetery, the land could have been cut and filled extensively and all clues to the real "Dragon" obliterated in the process.

Although these are valid arguments, it would be so much better to have a facing that satisfies both "Dragon" and water, if at all possible.[10]

At this point, I wish to address a common confusion in respect of tomb facing. According to certain fēngshuǐ schools, the Heaven Plate should be used to measure the facing[11]. This can be misleading. In the wider application of fēngshuǐ, the facing of a house or tomb is always measured using the Earth Plate, and any reference to a facing, unless otherwise qualified, is deemed to be an Earth Plate reading.

In case study #2 above, the tomb is always referred to as "sitting 壬 facing 丙" (Earth Plate readings), never "facing 巳", even though the tomb axis passes through the 巽巳 Paired-mountains on the Heaven Plate.

---

10 After all, sān hè fēngshuǐ is founded on the principle that the 3 factors "Dragon" water and facing should be so well coordinated that the site remains auspicious through the vagaries of time.

11 Indeed such a statement is even found in some classical texts, but on closer scrutiny, the statement was used in the context of matching facing to water flow. In that context the statement is not wrong, but it can be misleading if simply stated without qualification.

## Part-2: Setting up a Facing (立向)

No doubt the Heaven Plate is used to determine a given facing's conformity with the water requirements, but that is not the same as measuring the facing. Do not confuse yīn and yáng Earth Plate facings with yīn (right-to-left) and yáng (left-to-right) water flows.

The student should be clear on this, as otherwise his thinking could be clouded by the seemingly incompatible views of the different schools.

After resolving the "Dragon" and water requirements, it is also necessary to evaluate the effects of the Embraces (surrounding hills). Chp-2.5 discusses Embraces.

# CHAPTER-2.5
## Assessing the Embraces (撥砂法)

Part-2: Setting up a Facing (立向)

## CHAPTER-2.5
## Assessing the Embraces (撥砂法)

1. The method described herein is attributed to Grandmaster Lài Bù Yī (賴布衣) (12th Century CE). Only the mechanics of the steps are described here, but more info is provided in Appendix-2, just in case some readers want to probe deeper.

2. The purpose is to assess whether the prominent hills (and other tall edifices) around the tomb exert a beneficial or harmful effect on the tomb. For this purpose the "24-Mountains Human Plate (人盤中針)" is used (Fig-1 middle ring).

   This ring of the luó pán has a different distribution of the 5 elements amongst the 24 Mountains. They are called "Human Plate 5 Elements" (HP5E), as follows:

   子，午，卯，酉，甲，庚，丙，壬 – Fire

   乾，坤，艮，巽 – Wood

   乙，辛，丁，癸 – Earth

   辰，戌，丑，未 – Metal

   寅，申，巳，亥 – Water

   Do note that Mountains that are diametrically opposite each other have the same HP5E. In other words, a tomb axis will always have the same HP5E at both the sitting and the facing ends.

3. The Sitting Mountain of the tomb is always defined using the Earth Plate. After that has been established, look at the luó pán to see where the tomb axis falls on the the Human Plate, and determine the HP5E according to para 2 above.

# Part-2: Setting up a Facing (立向)

The Human Plate Mountain may or may not be the same as the Earth Plate Mountain. For example, If the tomb sits 子 faces 午 on the Earth Plate but the axis is tilted towards 癸/丁, then the tomb axis could in fact fall on 癸/丁 on the Human Plate. In such a case the HP5E of the tomb is Earth, not Fire.

4. Next stand at the tomb and measure the peaks of all prominent hills around the tomb using the Human Plate, and determine their respective HP5E according to para 2 above. All these hills are called Embraces.

    Technically, the all-important "Table Mountain" in front of the tomb is also an Embrace, although we do not usually measure it unless there are peaks protruding from the "Table Mountain".

5. Treating the tomb Sitting as the host and each Embrace as a guest, evaluate the elemental interaction between the host and each guest:

    | | |
    |---|---|
    | guest grows host (生砂) | |
    | guest prospers (same as) host (旺砂) | } positive interactions, friendly |
    | host counters guest (奴砂) | |

    | | |
    |---|---|
    | host grows guest (洩砂) (hence depleting the host) | } negative interactions, unfriendly |
    | guest counters host (煞砂) | |

6. The bigger the Embrace, the bigger impact it will deliver. The nearer the Embrace, the quicker will be its effect on the tomb.

Part-2: Setting up a Facing (立向)

7. Fig-10 illustrates an example where one Embrace is friendly to the tomb, another is not.

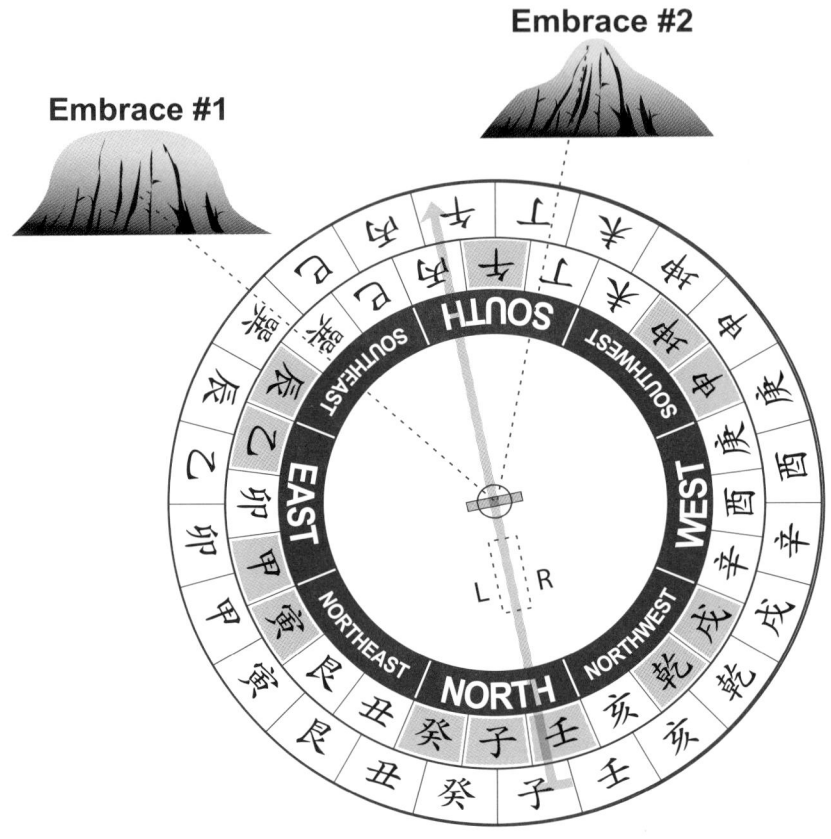

Tomb sitting 壬 (Earth Plate) penetrating Human Plate at 子, Human Plate Element = Fire host

Embrace #1 @ 巽 (Human Plate) H.P. Element = Wood guest grows host (生砂) hence friendly

Embrace #2 @ 丁 (Human Plate) H.P. Element = Earth guest depletes host (洩砂) hence unfriendly

**FIG-10: Assessing the Embraces**

8. The textbooks tell us to select a tomb axis, or tilt it, so that the majority of Embraces become friendly. In practice that is wishful thinking, for not only do we have to take care of the "Dragon" and water requirements, we also have to match the facing with the deceased's personal characteristics (Part-3). That leaves little scope for tweaking the tomb axis to accommodate the Embraces as well. Some suggestions are given in the Application Notes below.

## Application Notes

a. In practice, when there are multiple Embraces visible from a tomb, some are likely to be positively located, and others negative by this formula. It is only necessary to evaluate the 1 or 2 that are most significant by size or proximity. Otherwise, it can be a nightmare to try to sort out the lot.

b. Apart from its location, the shape of the Embrace also tells a story. A regularly shaped hill (pyramid, rounded or rectangular) is intrinsically beneficial, and will certainly be so if its location is positive. Likewise, a distorted or fragmented hill is intrinsically harmful and its negative attributes will no doubt be unleashed if its location is negative.

That begs the question: if there is an elegant hill at a negative location, is this hill harmful? By virtue of its positive shape (landform), the hill emits no shā qì. So it cannot be harmful even if it is negatively located (qì management factor). However its negative location means it is unfriendly to the host (the tomb). Hence its positive attributes are of no benefit to the tomb either.

## Part-2: Setting up a Facing (立向)

Similarly, an aggressive hill (landform factor) at a positive location (qì management factor) is friendly to the host (the tomb) and will hold its belligerence in check, but it does not have the wherewithal to do good either.

In general, landform (巒頭) factors have priority over qì management (理氣) factors such as those described in this handbook. This statement applies to all manner of landforms, not just Embraces.

c. What if the selected facing is compatible with the "Dragon" and water requirements but the major Embraces are unfriendly? Do we go ahead to use that facing anyway, or discard it and look for another?

My own view is that perfection is rare, almost impossible. Having favourable "Dragon" and water already qualifies the site as being superior. If some of the Embraces are unfriendly, it is comparable to a successful man having some small minded people around him waiting to stab him in the back. Should that stop the man from enjoying his success? It's a common enough situation in life, and the answer should be no different for a tomb facing that is short of perfection.

Moreover, just as in life, adversaries put us on guard, sharpen our fighting spirit. Likewise, a measure of unfriendly Embraces could in fact put some oomph into the tomb. [Think bā zì: a chart devoid of 7-Killings is unlikely to make a charismatic leader.]

Being able to establish a desirable facing based on "Dragon", water and Embraces is a vital step in yīn house fēngshuǐ, but it is not the end-game yet. It is just as important to personalize the facing to the deceased person's innate compatibilities. This topic is discussed in Part-3.

# Part-3

## Personalizing the Facing
(仙命宜忌)

# CHAPTER-3.1
## Principles

Part-3: Personalizing the Facing (仙命宜忌)

## CHAPTER-3.1
### Principles

A prospective burial plot may have excellent landform features, but it may not be compatible with the deceased person's natural inclinations, in which case the plot is deemed unsuitable for him in spite of the good landforms.

Part-3 hereof is about personalizing the tomb facing. This consideration is no less important than setting up a facing based on "Dragon" and water (Part-2). I mentioned in the preface that this book is a compilation of notes, and it just happened Part-2 was written earlier.

In practice it makes sense to check the user's compatibilities first before selecting a plot. Certain orientations are just not usable. So don't waste time even looking at those plots no matter how attractive otherwise.

A person's innate compatibilities are determined by his birth data. In analyzing the destiny of a living person, we have to consider his year, month, date and hour of birth – the so-called "4 Pillars (四柱)", or simply "bā zì (八字)". After the person has died, only his "Year Pillar (年柱)" remains relevant. [Note: year of birth, not death.] His compatibilities are determined by comparing his "Year Pillar" with the Sitting Mountain of the proposed tomb.[12]

---

12 The criteria are based on Branch interactions (地支生旺洩剋論), and also the nà yīn elemental (納音五行) interactions between the person's "Year Pillar" and the tomb's Sitting Mountain. However, the underlying theory will be skipped in this practical handbook. Only the results are tabulated.

# Part-3: Personalizing the Facing (仙命宜忌)

Please note that for compatibility deliberations, the Sitting Mountain of the tomb, i.e. the Mountain on the Earth Plate diametrically opposite the facing, becomes the reference parameter. This contrasts sharply with Part-2 where it is the facing that counts.

The traditional sān hè technique observed many taboos, to the extent that very few orientations were usable for any one person. In the old days, families that had the means enjoyed great leeway in locating their tombs. Wealthy families used to buy up large tracts of land in the wilderness and turned them into private burial grounds, and of course only the rich could afford fēngshuǐ masters. Within those private grounds, they had complete freedom to orientate a tomb any way they liked, and it was possible to avoid all of the prescribed taboos.

It is a very different story today. Firstly, modern burial grounds are strictly regulated by the government, and are often in short supply. Secondly, economic land usage within the publicly sanctioned burial grounds often imposes severe restrictions in terms of plot size and permissible orientations. If one were to observe all the traditional taboos rigidly, it would be very difficult indeed to find a usable plot, bearing in mind we also have to comply with the "Dragon" and water requirements described in Part-2.

Prioritization is clearly called for. Having studied the logic behind the taboos, I decided to separate them into 2 groups, "major" and "minor". The major taboos I would observe strictly, but am inclined to take a chance on the minors.

Part-3: Personalizing the Facing (仙命宜忌)

First, the "majors": bā zì students will have no difficulty recognizing these

a. "**Clash**" between Sitting Mountain and deceased's Year Branch (命冲)

| Deceased's Yr Branch | 子 | 丑 | 寅 | 卯 | 辰 | 巳 | 午 | 未 | 申 | 酉 | 戌 | 亥 |
|---|---|---|---|---|---|---|---|---|---|---|---|---|
| Sitting Mountain | 午 | 未 | 申 | 酉 | 戌 | 亥 | 子 | 丑 | 寅 | 卯 | 辰 | 巳 |

b. Sitting Mountain is one of the "3-**Killings**" group, including the 2 sandwiched Stems, affecting the deceased's Year Branch (命殺)

| Deceased's Yr Branch | 子 | 丑 | 寅 | 卯 | 辰 | 巳 | 午 | 未 | 申 | 酉 | 戌 | 亥 |
|---|---|---|---|---|---|---|---|---|---|---|---|---|
| Sitting Mountain | 巳丙午丁未 | 寅甲卯乙辰 | 亥壬子癸丑 | 申庚酉辛戌 | 巳丙午丁未 | 寅甲卯乙辰 | 亥壬子癸丑 | 申庚酉辛戌 | 巳丙午丁未 | 寅甲卯乙辰 | 亥壬子癸丑 | 申庚酉辛戌 |

# Part-3: Personalizing the Facing (仙命宜忌)

c. Sitting Mountain represents the "**Direct Killing**" of the deceased's Year Branch (正殺)

| Deceased's Yr Branch | 子 | 丑 | 寅 | 卯 | 辰 | 巳 | 午 | 未 | 申 | 酉 | 戌 | 亥 |
|---|---|---|---|---|---|---|---|---|---|---|---|---|
| Sitting Mountain | 未 | 辰 | 丑 | 戌 | 未 | 辰 | 丑 | 戌 | 未 | 辰 | 丑 | 戌 |

Actually, the "Direct Killing" is already a component of the "3-Killings" in item-b above. It is emphasized here because it is regarded as the fiercest, and the most insidious, of them all. Being Earth Mountains, 辰戌丑未 retain the strongest energies.

The conservative view is that even if the tomb sits on an adjacent Mountain but the tomb axis passes within 3° of the "Direct Killing" Mountain, it would constitute a violation. I find this overly restrictive and am prepared to overlook it if choices are limited in practice.

d. Sitting Mountain "**Punishes**" the Year Branch, and vice-versa (命刑)

| Deceased's Yr Branch | 子 | 丑 | 寅 | 卯 | 辰 | 巳 | 午 | 未 | 申 | 酉 | 戌 | 亥 |
|---|---|---|---|---|---|---|---|---|---|---|---|---|
| Sitting Mountain | 卯 | 戌,(未) | 巳,(申) | 子 | 辰 | 寅,申 | 午 | 戌,(丑) | 巳,(寅) | 酉 | 丑,未 | 亥 |

The Mountains within parenthesis are "Clashes" as well as "Punishments". So they have already been taken into account in item-a above.

## Part-3: Personalizing the Facing (仙命宜忌)

### e. Sitting Mountain "**Seated**" on Year Branch (命坐)

| Deceased's Yr Branch | 子 | 丑 | 寅 | 卯 | 辰 | 巳 | 午 | 未 | 申 | 酉 | 戌 | 亥 |
|---|---|---|---|---|---|---|---|---|---|---|---|---|
| Sitting Mountain | 子 | 丑 | 寅 | 卯 | 辰 | 巳 | 午 | 未 | 申 | 酉 | 戌 | 亥 |

It may seem strange that a Sitting Mountain that co-prospers with one's own Year Branch is deemed negative, but by the ancient "Gods & Killings" system (神煞論), this Mountain represents the "Burying Child Gate (埋兒關煞)", and is thus to be avoided for the wellbeing of one's descendants.

### f. Sitting Mountain "**Harms**" the Year Branch (命害)

| Deceased's Yr Branch | 子 | 丑 | 寅 | 卯 | 辰 | 巳 | 午 | 未 | 申 | 酉 | 戌 | 亥 |
|---|---|---|---|---|---|---|---|---|---|---|---|---|
| Sitting Mountain | 未 | 午 | 巳 | 辰 | 卯 | 寅 | 丑 | 子 | 亥 | 戌 | 酉 | 申 |

The "minor" taboos are named below, but I would not be defining each of them, suffice to say that the demerits they carry are less severe than the "majors" listed above, and may be mitigated by judicious selection of final tomb axis down to "Gold Divisions" (Chp-3.3) and date selection (Part-5).

- "**Retreat**" (命退)
- "**3-Combo**" (三合喪)
- "**Summons**" (官符)
- "**Grotto**" (喪窟)
- "**Pit**" (喪坑)
- "**Piercing Harm**" (刺害煞)

# Part-3: Personalizing the Facing (仙命宜忌)

The above taboos, Major and Minor, are tabulated in Chapter-3.2 for each of the 60 possible Year Pillars. The last row in each table marks the Sitting Mountains that are free of all taboos.

If the client is lucky enough to find a plot that sits on a taboo free Mountain, and still complies with the "Dragon" and water requirements discussed in Part-2 hereof, that plot is the obvious choice. But such happy coincidences are few and far in between. More often than not, we have to contend with less than perfect scenarios. This is where the skill and experience of the fēngshuǐ master is called upon to find the optimum plot and orientation given the practical limitations.

# CHAPTER-3.2
## Compatibility Tables

# Part-3: Personalizing the Facing (仙命宜忌)

## CHAPTER-3.2
### Compatibility Tables

**Year Pillar:** 甲子 (1864, 1924, 1984, 2044…)  **nà yīn element:** Metal

**Sitting Mountain**

| | 壬子 | 癸丑 | 艮寅 | 甲卯 | 乙辰 | 巽巳 | 丙午 | 丁未 | 坤申 | 庚酉 | 辛戌 | 乾亥 |
|---|---|---|---|---|---|---|---|---|---|---|---|---|
| **Clash** | | | | | | | ● | | | | | |
| **Killings** | | | | | | | ● | ● | | | | |
| **Direct K** | | | | | | ● | ● | ● | | | | |
| **Punish** | | | | ● | | | | | | | | |
| **Seated** | ● | | | | | | | | | | | |
| **Harm** | | | | | | | | ● | | | | |
| **Retreat** | ○ | ○ | ○ | ○ | ○ | | | | | | | |
| **3-Combo** | | | | | ○ | | | | | | | |
| **Summons** | | | | | | | | | | ○ | | |
| **Grotto** | ○ | | | | | | | | | | | |
| **Pit** | | | | ○ | | | | | | | | |
| **Piercing H** | | | | | | ○ | ○ | ○ | | | | |
| **Free** | | | | | | | | ✓ | | ✓ | ✓ | ✓ |

● major    ○ minor    ✓ taboo free

# Part-3: Personalizing the Facing (仙命宜忌)

**Year Pillar: 乙丑 (1865, 1925, 1985, 2045…)    nà yīn element: Metal**

**Sitting Mountain**

| | 壬 | 子 | 癸 | 丑 | 艮 | 寅 | 甲 | 卯 | 乙 | 辰 | 巽 | 巳 | 丙 | 午 | 丁 | 未 | 坤 | 申 | 庚 | 酉 | 辛 | 戌 | 乾 | 亥 |
|---|---|---|---|---|---|---|---|---|---|---|---|---|---|---|---|---|---|---|---|---|---|---|---|---|
| Clash | | | | | | | | | | | | | | | | | | | | | | | | |
| Killings | | | | ● | ● | ● | ● | ● | | | | | | | | | | | | | | | | |
| Direct K | | | | | | | | | | ● | | | | | | | | | | | | | | |
| Punish | | | | | | | | | | | | | | | | | | | | | | ● | | |
| Seated | | | | ● | | | | | | | | | | | | | | | | | | | | |
| Harm | | | | | | | | | | | | | | | | ● | | | | | | | | |
| Retreat | ○ | ○ | ○ | | | | | | | | | | | | | | | | | | | ○ | ○ | ○ |
| 3-Combo | | | | | | | | | | | | ○ | | | | | | | | ○ | | | | |
| Summons | | | | | | | | | | | | | | | | | | ○ | | | | | | |
| Grotto | | ○ | | | | | | | | | | | | | | | | | | | | | | |
| Pit | | | | | ○ | | | | | | | | | | | | | | | | | | | |
| Piercing H | | | | | | | | | | | | ○ | ○ | ○ | | | | | | | ○ | | | |
| Free | | | | | | | | | | | ✓ | | | | | | | | ✓ | | ✓ | | ✓ | |

● major    ○ minor    ✓ taboo free

# Part-3: Personalizing the Facing (仙命宜忌)

**Year Pillar:** 丙寅 (1866, 1926, 1986, 2046…)    **nà yīn element:** Fire

| | Sitting Mountain | | | | | | | | | | | | | | | | | | | | | | | |
|---|---|---|---|---|---|---|---|---|---|---|---|---|---|---|---|---|---|---|---|---|---|---|---|---|
| | 壬 | 子 | 癸 | 丑 | 艮 | 寅 | 甲 | 卯 | 乙 | 辰 | 巽 | 巳 | 丙 | 午 | 丁 | 未 | 坤 | 申 | 庚 | 酉 | 辛 | 戌 | 乾 | 亥 |
| **Clash** | | | | | | | | | | | | | | | | | | ● | | | | | | |
| **Killings** | | ● | | ● | | | | | | | | | | | | | | | | | | ● | | ● |
| **Direct K** | | ● | | | | | | | | | | | | | | | | | | | | | | |
| **Punish** | | | | | | | | | | | | ● | | | | | | | | | | | | |
| **Seated** | | | | | ● | | | | | | | | | | | | | | | | | | | |
| **Harm** | | | | | | | | | | | | ● | | | ● | | | | | | | | | |
| **Retreat** | | | | | | | ○ | | ○ | ○ | ○ | | | | | ○ | | | | | | | | |
| **3-Combo** | | | | | | | | | | | | | | ○ | | | | | | | | ○ | | |
| **Summons** | | | | | | | | | | | | | ○ | | | | | | | | | | | |
| **Grotto** | | | | ○ | | | | | | | | | | | | | | | | | | | | |
| **Pit** | | | | | | | | | ○ | | | | | | | | | | | | | | | |
| **Piercing H** | ○ | ○ | | | | | | | | | | | | | | | | | | | | | | |
| **Free** | | | | | | | | ✓ | ✓ | ✓ | ✓ | | ✓ | | ✓ | | | | | | | | ✓ | |

● major    ○ minor    ✓ taboo free

# Part-3: Personalizing the Facing (仙命宜忌)

**Year Pillar:** 丁卯 (1867, 1927, 1987, 2047…)    **nà yīn element: Fire**

**Sitting Mountain**

| | 壬 | 子 | 癸 | 丑 | 艮 | 寅 | 甲 | 卯 | 乙 | 辰 | 巽 | 巳 | 丙 | 午 | 丁 | 未 | 坤 | 申 | 庚 | 酉 | 辛 | 戌 | 乾 | 亥 |
|---|---|---|---|---|---|---|---|---|---|---|---|---|---|---|---|---|---|---|---|---|---|---|---|---|
| **Clash** | | | | | | | | | | | | | | | | | | | | | | | | |
| **Killings** | | | | | | | | | | | | | | | | | | | ● | ● | ● | | | |
| **Direct K** | | | | | | | | | | | | | | | | | | | | ● | ● | ● | | |
| **Punish** | | | | ● | | | | | | | | | | | | | | | | | | | | |
| **Seated** | | | | | | | | ● | | | | | | | | | | | | | | | | |
| **Harm** | | | | | | | | | | ● | | | | | | | | | | | | | | |
| **Retreat** | | | | | | | | | | ○ | ○ | ○ | ○ | ○ | | | | | | | | | | |
| **3-Combo** | | | | | | | | | | | | | | | | ○ | | | | | | | | |
| **Summons** | | | | | | ○ | | | | | | | | | | | | | | | | | | |
| **Grotto** | | | | | | | | ○ | | | | | | | | | | | | | | | | |
| **Pit** | | | | | | | | | | | | ○ | | | | | | | | | | | | |
| **Piercing H** | ○ | ○ | ○ | | | | | | | | | | | | | | | | | | | | | |
| **Free** | | ✓ | ✓ | | | | | | | | | | | | | | | | | | | ✓ | | ✓ |

● major    ○ minor    ✓ taboo free

# Part-3: Personalizing the Facing (仙命宜忌)

**Year Pillar: 戊辰 (1868, 1928, 1988, 2048…)  nà yīn element: Wood**

**Sitting Mountain**

| | 壬 | 子 | 癸 | 丑 | 艮 | 寅 | 甲 | 卯 | 乙 | 辰 | 巽 | 巳 | 丙 | 午 | 丁 | 未 | 坤 | 申 | 庚 | 酉 | 辛 | 戌 | 乾 | 亥 |
|---|---|---|---|---|---|---|---|---|---|---|---|---|---|---|---|---|---|---|---|---|---|---|---|---|
| Clash | | | | | | | | | | | | | | | | | | | | | | ● | | |
| Killings | | | | | | | | | | | | ● | ● | ● | ● | | | | | | | | | |
| Direct K | | | | | | | | | | | | | ● | | | | | | | | | | | |
| Punish | | | | | | | | | ● | ● | | | | | | | | | | | | | | |
| Seated | | | | | | | | | | ● | | | | | | | | | | | | | | |
| Harm | | | | | | | ● | | | | | | | | | | | | | | | | | |
| Retreat | | | ○ | ○ | ○ | ○ | ○ | ○ | | | | | | | | | | | | | | | | |
| 3-Combo | ○ | | | | | | | | | | | | | | | | | | | | | | | |
| Summons | | | | | | | | | | ○ | | | | | | | | | | | | | | ○ |
| Grotto | | | | | | | | | | | | ○ | | | | | | | | | | | | |
| Pit | | | | | | | | | | | | | | | | | ○ | | | | | | | |
| Piercing H | | | | | | | | | | | | | | | | | | | ○ | ○ | ○ | ○ | ○ | |
| Free | ✓ | ✓ | | | | | | | | | | | | | | | ✓ | | | | | | | |

● major   ○ minor   ✓ taboo free

# Part-3: Personalizing the Facing (仙命宜忌)

**Year Pillar:** 己巳 (1869, 1929, 1989, 2049…)  **nà yīn element:** Wood

## Sitting Mountain

| | 壬 | 子 | 癸 | 丑 | 艮 | 寅 | 甲 | 卯 | 乙 | 辰 | 巽 | 巳 | 丙 | 午 | 丁 | 未 | 坤 | 申 | 庚 | 酉 | 辛 | 戌 | 乾 | 亥 |
|---|---|---|---|---|---|---|---|---|---|---|---|---|---|---|---|---|---|---|---|---|---|---|---|---|
| Clash | | | | | | | | | | | | | | | | | | | | | | | | ● |
| Killings | | | | | | ● | | ● | ● | ● | | | | | | | | | | | | | | |
| Direct K | | | | | | | | | | ● | | | | | | | | | | | | | | |
| Punish | | | | | | ● | | | | | | | ● | | | | | | | | | | | |
| Seated | | | | | | | | | | | | | | | ● | | | | | | | | | |
| Harm | | | | | | ● | | | | | | | | | | | | | | | | | | |
| Retreat | ○ | ○ | ○ | | | | | | | | | | | | | | | | | | | | | |
| 3-Combo | | | | ○ | | | | | | | | | | | | | | | | | | | | |
| Summons | | | | | | | | | | | | | | | | | | | | ○ | | | | |
| Grotto | | | | | | | | | | | | ○ | | | | | | | | | | | | |
| Pit | | | | | | | | | | | | | | ○ | | | | | | | | | | |
| Piercing H | | | | | | | | | | | | | | | | | | ○ | ○ | ○ | ○ | ○ | ○ | ○ |
| Free | | | | ✓ | | | | | | | | | | | | ✓ | ✓ | ✓ | | | | | | |

● major   ○ minor   ✓ taboo free

# Part-3: Personalizing the Facing (仙命宜忌)

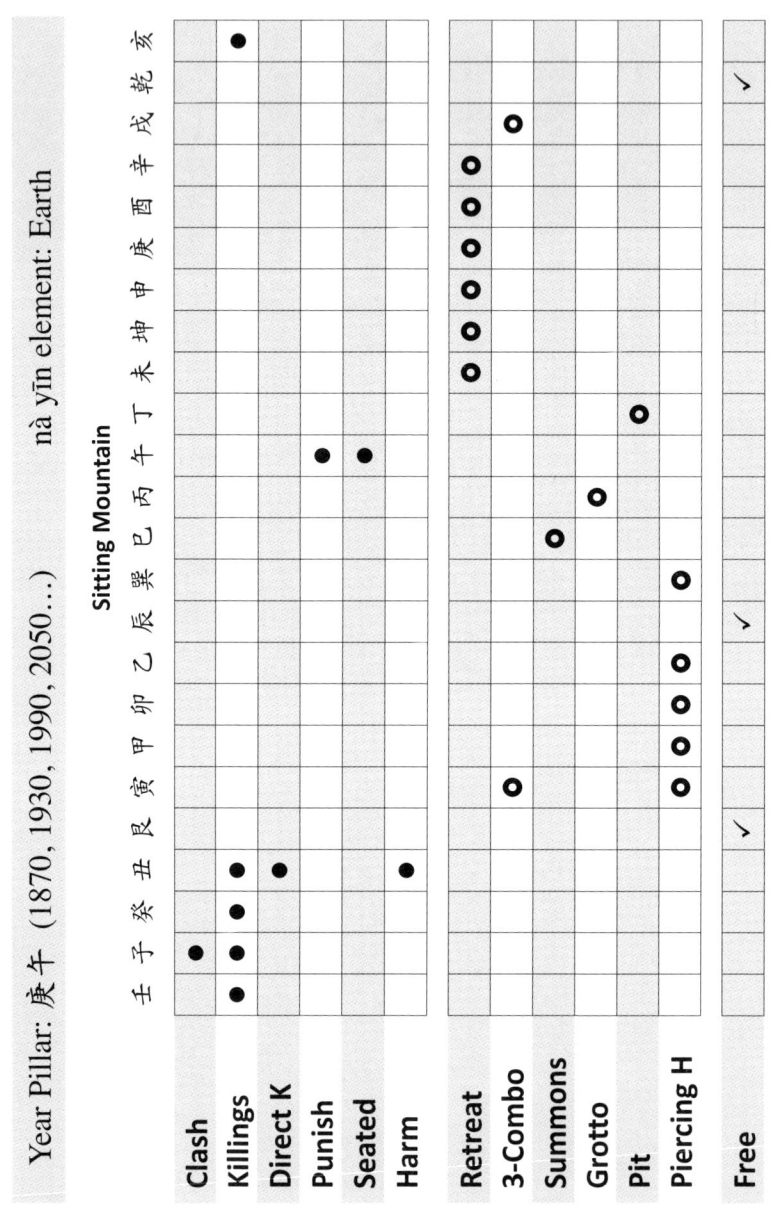

# Part-3: Personalizing the Facing (仙命宜忌)

**Year Pillar: 辛未 (1871, 1931, 1991, 2051…)**

**nà yīn element: Earth**

## Sitting Mountain

| | 壬 | 子 | 癸 | 丑 | 艮 | 寅 | 甲 | 卯 | 乙 | 辰 | 巽 | 巳 | 丙 | 午 | 丁 | 未 | 坤 | 申 | 庚 | 酉 | 辛 | 戌 | 乾 | 亥 |
|---|---|---|---|---|---|---|---|---|---|---|---|---|---|---|---|---|---|---|---|---|---|---|---|---|
| Clash | | | | • | | | | | | | | | | | | | | | | | | | | |
| Killings | | | | | | | | | | | | | | | | | | | | • | • | • | | |
| Direct K | | | | | | | | | | | | | | | | | | | | | | • | | |
| Punish | | | | | | | • | | | | | | | | | | | | | | | • | | |
| Seated | | | | | | | | | | | | | | | | • | | | | | | | | |
| Harm | | • | | | | | | | | | | | | | | | | | | | | | | |
| Retreat | | | | | | | | | | | | | ○ | ○ | ○ | ○ | | | | | | | | |
| 3-Combo | | | | | | | | ○ | | | | | | | | | | | | | | | | |
| Summons | | | | | | ○ | | | | | | | | | | | | | ○ | | | | | |
| Grotto | | | | | | | | | | | | | | | | | | | | | ○ | | | |
| Pit | | | | | | | | | ○ | ○ | ○ | ○ | | | | | | | | | | | | |
| Piercing H | | | | | | | | | | | | | | | | | | ○ | | | | | | |
| Free | ✓ | ✓ | | | | | | | | | | | | | | | | | | | | | | ✓ |

● major  ○ minor  ✓ taboo free

# Part-3: Personalizing the Facing (仙命宜忌)

**Year Pillar: 壬申 (1872, 1932, 1992, 2052…)**　　　　nà yīn element: Metal

### Sitting Mountain

| | 壬 | 子 | 癸 | 丑 | 艮 | 寅 | 甲 | 卯 | 乙 | 辰 | 巽 | 巳 | 丙 | 午 | 丁 | 未 | 坤 | 申 | 庚 | 酉 | 辛 | 戌 | 乾 | 亥 |
|---|---|---|---|---|---|---|---|---|---|---|---|---|---|---|---|---|---|---|---|---|---|---|---|---|
| **Clash** | | | | | ● | | | | | | | | | | | | | | | | | | | |
| **Killings** | | | | | | | | | | | | ● | ● | ● | ● | | | | | | | | | |
| **Direct K** | | | | | | | | | | | | | ● | | | | | | | | | | | |
| **Punish** | | | | | | | | | | | ● | | | | | | | | | | | | | |
| **Seated** | | | | | | | | | | | | | | | | | | ● | | | | | | |
| **Harm** | | | | | | | | | | | | | | | | | | | | | | | | ● |
| **Retreat** | | ○ | ○ | ○ | ○ | ○ | ○ | | | | | | | | | | | | | | | | | |
| **3-Combo** | | ○ | | | | | | | | | | | | | | | | | | | | | | |
| **Summons** | | | | | | | | | | ○ | | | | | | | | | | | | | | ○ |
| **Grotto** | | | | | | | | | | | | | | | | | ○ | | | | | | | |
| **Pit** | | | | | | | | | | | | | | | | | | | | ○ | | | | |
| **Piercing H** | | | | | | | | | | | | ○ | ○ | ○ | | | | | | | | | | |
| **Free** | ✓ | ✓ | | | | | | | | | | | | | | | | | | | ✓ | ✓ | ✓ | ✓ |

● major　○ minor　✓ taboo free

# Part-3: Personalizing the Facing (仙命宜忌)

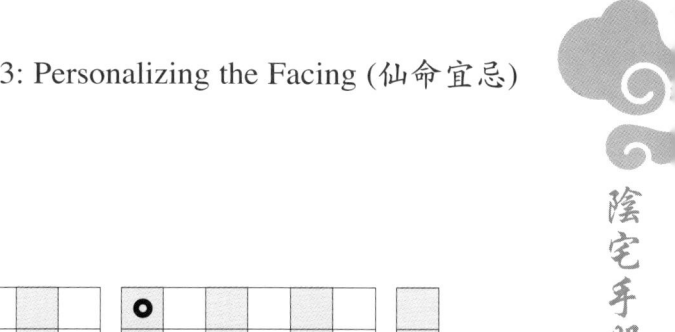

**Year Pillar:** 癸酉 (1873, 1933, 1993, 2053…)    **nà yīn element:** Metal

### Sitting Mountain

| | 壬 | 子 | 癸 | 丑 | 艮 | 寅 | 甲 | 卯 | 乙 | 辰 | 巽 | 巳 | 丙 | 午 | 丁 | 未 | 坤 | 申 | 庚 | 酉 | 辛 | 戌 | 乾 | 亥 |
|---|---|---|---|---|---|---|---|---|---|---|---|---|---|---|---|---|---|---|---|---|---|---|---|---|
| Clash | | | | | | | | ● | | | | | | | | | | | | | | | | |
| Killings | | | | | | ● | ● | ● | ● | | | | | | | | | | | | | | | |
| Direct K | | | | | | | | ● | | | | | | | | | | | | | | | | |
| Punish | | | | | | | | | | | | | | | | | | | | ● | | | | |
| Seated | | | | | | | | | | | | | | | | | | | | | | ● | | |
| Harm | | | | | | | | | | | | | ● | ● | | | | | | | | | | |
| Retreat | ○ | ○ | ○ | | | | | | | | | | | | | | | | | | | | | |
| 3-Combo | | | | ○ | | | | | | | | | | | | | | | | | | | | |
| Summons | | | | | | | | | | | | | | | ○ | | | | | | | | | |
| Grotto | | | | | | | | | | | | | | | | | | ○ | | | | | | |
| Pit | | | | | | | | | | | | | ○ | | | | | | | | | | | |
| Piercing H | | | | | | | | | | | | ○ | ○ | ○ | | | | | | | ○ | | | |
| Free | | | | | | | | | | | ✓ | | | | | | | | | | | | ✓ | ✓ |

● major    ○ minor    ✓ taboo free

# Part-3: Personalizing the Facing (仙命宜忌)

Year Pillar: 甲戌 (1874, 1934, 1994, 2054...)   nà yīn element: Fire

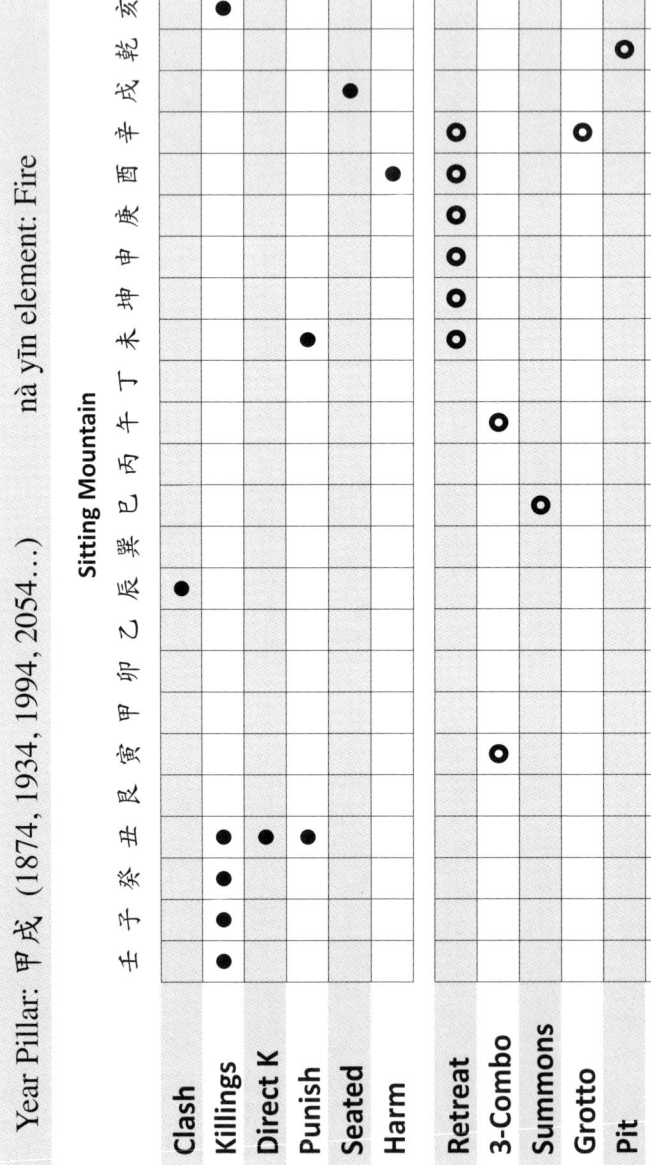

● major   ○ minor   ✓ taboo free

# Part-3: Personalizing the Facing (仙命宜忌)

**Year Pillar: 乙亥 (1875, 1935, 1995, 2055…)    nà yīn element: Fire**

## Sitting Mountain

| | 壬 | 子 | 癸 | 丑 | 艮 | 寅 | 甲 | 卯 | 乙 | 辰 | 巽 | 巳 | 丙 | 午 | 丁 | 未 | 坤 | 申 | 庚 | 酉 | 辛 | 戌 | 乾 | 亥 |
|---|---|---|---|---|---|---|---|---|---|---|---|---|---|---|---|---|---|---|---|---|---|---|---|---|
| Clash | | | | | | | | | | | | ● | | | | | | | | | | | | |
| Killings | | | | | | ● | ● | ● | | | | | | | | | | | | | | | | |
| Direct K | | | | | | | | | | | | | | | | | | | | | | ● | | |
| Punish | | | | | | | | | | | | | | | | | | | ● | | | ● | | |
| Seated | | | | | | | | | | | | | | | | | | | | | | ● | | ● |
| Harm | | | | | | | | | | | | | | | | | | ● | | | | | | |
| Retreat | | | | | | | | | | ○ | ○ | ○ | ○ | ○ | | | | | | | | | | |
| 3-Combo | | | | | | | | ○ | | | | | | | ○ | | | | | | | | | |
| Summons | | | | | | ○ | | | | | | | | | | | | | | | | | | |
| Grotto | | | | | | | | | | | | | | | | | | | | ○ | | | | |
| Pit | ○ | | | | | | | | | | | | | | | | | | | | | | | |
| Piercing H | | ○ | ○ | ○ | | | | | | | | | | | | | | | | | | | | |
| Free | | | | ✓ | ✓ | ✓ | | | ✓ | ✓ | | | | | | | | | | | | ✓ | | |

● major   ○ minor   ✓ taboo free

The yīn House Handbook

# Part-3: Personalizing the Facing (仙命宜忌)

**Year Pillar:** 丙子 (1876, 1936, 1996, 2056…)　　　nà yīn element: Water

**Sitting Mountain**

| | 壬 | 子 | 癸 | 丑 | 艮 | 寅 | 甲 | 卯 | 乙 | 辰 | 巽 | 巳 | 丙 | 午 | 丁 | 未 | 坤 | 申 | 庚 | 酉 | 辛 | 戌 | 乾 | 亥 |
|---|---|---|---|---|---|---|---|---|---|---|---|---|---|---|---|---|---|---|---|---|---|---|---|---|
| Clash | | | | | | | | | | | | | | | | | | | | | | | | |
| Killings | | | | | | | | | | | | ● | ● | ● | | ● | | | | | | | | |
| Direct K | | | | | | | | | | | | | ● | | | | | | | | | | | |
| Punish | | | | | | | ● | | | | | | | | | | | | | | | | | |
| Seated | ● | | | | | | | | | | | | | | | | | | | | | | | |
| Harm | | | | | | | | | | | | | | | ● | | | | | | | | | |
| Retreat | | | ○ | ○ | ○ | ○ | ○ | | | | | | | | | | | | | | | | | |
| 3-Combo | | | | | | | | | | ○ | | | | | | | | ○ | | | | | | |
| Summons | | | | | | | | | | | | | | | | | | | | | | | ○ | |
| Grotto | ○ | | | | | | | | | | | | | | | | | | | | | | | |
| Pit | | | ○ | | | | | | | | | | | | | | | | | | | | | |
| Piercing H | | | ○ | ○ | | | | | | | | | | | | | | ○ | ○ | | | ○ | | |
| Free | | | | | | | | | | | | | | ✓ | | | | | | ✓ | ✓ | ✓ | | ✓ |

● major　○ minor　✓ taboo free

# Part-3: Personalizing the Facing (仙命宜忌)

**Year Pillar:** 丁丑 (1877, 1937, 1997, 2057…)     **nà yīn element:** Water

**Sitting Mountain**

| | 壬 | 子 | 癸 | 丑 | 艮 | 寅 | 甲 | 卯 | 乙 | 辰 | 巽 | 巳 | 丙 | 午 | 丁 | 未 | 坤 | 申 | 庚 | 酉 | 辛 | 戌 | 乾 | 亥 |
|---|---|---|---|---|---|---|---|---|---|---|---|---|---|---|---|---|---|---|---|---|---|---|---|---|
| Clash | | | | | | | | | | | | | | | | ● | | | | | | | | |
| Killings | | | | | ● | ● | ● | ● | ● | | | | | | | | | | | | | | | |
| Direct K | | | | | | | | ● | | ● | | | | | | | | | | | | | | |
| Punish | | | | | | | | | | | | | | | | | | | | | | ● | | |
| Seated | | | | ● | | | | | | | | | | | | | | | | | | | | |
| Harm | | | | | | | | | | | | | | ● | | | | | | | | | | |
| Retreat | ● | ○ | | | | | | | | | | | | | | | | | | | | | | |
| 3-Combo | | | | | | | | | | | | ○ | | | | | | | | ○ | | | | |
| Summons | | | | | | | | | | | | | | | | | | ○ | | | | | | |
| Grotto | | | ○ | | | | | | | | | | | | | | | | | | | | | |
| Pit | | | | ○ | | | | | | | | | | | | | | | | | | | | |
| Piercing H | | | | | | | | | | ○ | | | | | | ○ | ○ | | | | | ○ | | |
| Free | | | | | ✓ | | | | | | ✓ | | | | ✓ | | ✓ | | | | ✓ | | | |

● major    ○ minor    ✓ taboo free

# Part-3: Personalizing the Facing (仙命宜忌)

**Year Pillar:** 戊寅 (1878, 1938, 1998, 2058…)   **nà yīn element:** Earth

### Sitting Mountain

| | 壬 | 子 | 癸 | 丑 | 艮 | 寅 | 甲 | 卯 | 乙 | 辰 | 巽 | 巳 | 丙 | 午 | 丁 | 未 | 坤 | 申 | 庚 | 酉 | 辛 | 戌 | 乾 | 亥 | Free |
|---|---|---|---|---|---|---|---|---|---|---|---|---|---|---|---|---|---|---|---|---|---|---|---|---|---|
| Clash | | | | | | | | | | | | | | | | | | ● | | | | | | | |
| Killings | ● | ● | ● | ● | | | | | | | | | | | | | | | | | | | | | |
| Direct K | | | | ● | | | | | | | | | | | | | | | | | | | | | |
| Punish | | | | | | | | | | | | ● | | | | | | | | | | | | | |
| Seated | | | | | | ● | | | | | | | | | | | | | | | | | | | |
| Harm | | | | | | | | | | | | ● | | | | | | | | | | | | | |
| Retreat | | | | | | | | | | | | | | | | ○ | ○ | ○ | ○ | ○ | ○ | | | | |
| 3-Combo | | | | | | | | | | | | | | ○ | | | | | | | | ○ | | | |
| Summons | | | | | | | | | | | | ○ | | | | | | | | | | | | | |
| Grotto | | | | | | | | | ○ | | | | | | | | | | | | | | | | |
| Pit | | | | | | | ○ | ○ | | | | | | | | | | | | | | | | | |
| Piercing H | | | | | ○ | ○ | ○ | | | | | | | | | | | | | | | | | | |
| Free | | | | | | | | | | ✓ | | | | | ✓ | | | | | | | | | ✓ | ✓ |

● major   ○ minor   ✓ taboo free

# Part-3: Personalizing the Facing (仙命宜忌)

**Year Pillar:** 己卯 (1879, 1939, 1999, 2059...)    **nà yīn element:** Earth

### Sitting Mountain

| | 壬 | 子 | 癸 | 丑 | 艮 | 寅 | 甲 | 卯 | 乙 | 辰 | 巽 | 巳 | 丙 | 午 | 丁 | 未 | 坤 | 申 | 庚 | 酉 | 辛 | 戌 | 乾 | 亥 |
|---|---|---|---|---|---|---|---|---|---|---|---|---|---|---|---|---|---|---|---|---|---|---|---|---|
| **Clash** | | | | | | | | | | | | | | | | | | | | | | | | |
| **Killings** | | | | | | | | | | | | | | | | | | | | ● | | ● | | |
| **Direct K** | | | | | | | | | | | | | | | | | | | | ● | | | | |
| **Punish** | | | | | | ● | | | | | | | | | | | | | | | | | | |
| **Seated** | | | | | | | | ● | | | | | | | | | | | | | | | | |
| **Harm** | | | | | | | | | | ● | | | | | | | | | | | | | | |
| **Retreat** | | | | | | | | | | ○ | ○ | ○ | ○ | ○ | ○ | | | | | | | | | |
| **3-Combo** | | | | | | | | | | | | | | | | ○ | | | | | | | | ○ |
| **Summons** | | | | | | ○ | | | | | | | | | | | | | | | | | | |
| **Grotto** | | | | | | | ○ | | | | | | | | | | | | | | | | | |
| **Pit** | | | | | | | | | ○ | ○ | | | | | | | | | | | | | | |
| **Piercing H** | | | | ○ | | | ○ | ○ | ○ | | ○ | | | | | | | | | | | | | |
| **Free** | | ✓ | ✓ | ✓ | | | | | | | | | | | | | | | | | ✓ | | ✓ | |

● major    ○ minor    ✓ taboo free

# Part-3: Personalizing the Facing (仙命宜忌)

**Year Pillar:** 庚辰 (1880, 1940, 2000, 2060…)   **nà yīn element: Metal**

### Sitting Mountain

|  | 壬 | 子 | 癸 | 丑 | 艮 | 寅 | 甲 | 卯 | 乙 | 辰 | 巽 | 巳 | 丙 | 午 | 丁 | 未 | 坤 | 申 | 庚 | 酉 | 辛 | 戌 | 乾 | 亥 |
|---|---|---|---|---|---|---|---|---|---|---|---|---|---|---|---|---|---|---|---|---|---|---|---|---|
| Clash |  |  |  |  |  |  |  |  |  |  |  |  |  |  |  |  |  |  |  |  |  | ● |  |  |
| Killings |  |  |  |  |  |  |  |  |  |  |  |  |  |  |  |  |  |  |  |  |  |  |  |  |
| Direct K |  |  |  |  |  |  |  |  |  |  |  | ● | ● | ● | ● |  |  |  |  |  |  |  |  |  |
| Punish |  |  |  |  |  |  |  |  |  |  |  |  |  |  |  |  |  |  |  |  |  |  |  |  |
| Seated |  |  |  |  |  |  |  |  |  | ● |  |  |  |  |  |  |  |  |  |  |  |  |  |  |
| Harm |  |  |  |  |  |  |  | ● |  |  |  |  |  |  |  |  |  |  |  |  |  |  |  |  |
| Retreat |  |  |  | ○ | ○ | ○ | ○ | ○ |  | ○ |  |  |  |  |  |  |  |  |  |  |  |  |  |  |
| 3-Combo |  | ○ |  |  |  |  |  |  |  |  |  |  |  |  |  |  |  |  |  |  |  |  |  |  |
| Summons |  |  |  |  |  |  |  |  |  |  |  |  |  |  |  |  |  | ○ |  |  |  |  |  |  |
| Grotto |  |  |  |  |  |  |  |  |  |  | ○ |  |  |  |  |  |  |  |  |  |  |  |  |  |
| Pit |  |  |  |  |  |  |  |  |  |  |  |  |  | ○ ○ ○ ○ |  |  |  |  |  |  |  |  |  |  |
| Piercing H |  |  |  |  |  |  |  |  |  |  | ○ ○ ○ ○ |  |  |  |  |  |  |  |  |  |  |  |  |  |
| Free | ✓ | ✓ |  |  |  |  |  |  |  |  |  |  |  |  |  | ✓ |  |  | ✓ | ✓ | ✓ |  | ✓ | ✓ |

● major    ○ minor    ✓ taboo free

# Part-3: Personalizing the Facing (仙命宜忌)

**Year Pillar: 辛巳 (1881, 1941, 2001, 2061…)   nà yīn element: Metal**

### Sitting Mountain

| | 壬 | 子 | 癸 | 丑 | 艮 | 寅 | 甲 | 卯 | 乙 | 辰 | 巽 | 巳 | 丙 | 午 | 丁 | 未 | 坤 | 申 | 庚 | 酉 | 辛 | 戌 | 乾 | 亥 |
|---|---|---|---|---|---|---|---|---|---|---|---|---|---|---|---|---|---|---|---|---|---|---|---|---|
| Clash | | | | | | | | | | | | | | | | | | | | | | | | ● |
| Killings | | | | | ● | ● | | ● | | ● | | | | | | | | | | | | | | |
| Direct K | | | | | | | | ● | | | | | | | | | | | | | | | | |
| Punish | | | | | | | | | | | | | | | | | | ● | | | | | | |
| Seated | | | | | | | | | | | | ● | | | | | | | | | | | | |
| Harm | | | | | | ● | | | | | | | | | | | | | | | | | | |
| Retreat | ○ | ○ | ○ | | | | | | | | | | | | | | | | | | | | | |
| 3-Combo | | | | ○ | | | | | | | | | | | | | | | | | | | | |
| Summons | | | | | | | | | | | | | | | | | | | | | | | | |
| Grotto | | | | | | | | | | | | | | | | | | | | ○ | | | | |
| Pit | | | | | | | | | | | | | ○ | | | | | | | | | | | |
| Piercing H | | | | | | | | | | | | | ○ | ○ | ○ | | | | | | | | | |
| Free | | | | | | | ✓ | | | | | | | | | ✓ | ✓ | | | | ✓ | | | |

● major    ○ minor    ✓ taboo free

# Part-3: Personalizing the Facing (仙命宜忌)

**Year Pillar:** 壬午 (1882, 1942, 2002, 2062…)    **nà yīn element:** Wood

**Sitting Mountain**

| | 壬 | 子 | 癸 | 丑 | 艮 | 寅 | 甲 | 卯 | 乙 | 辰 | 巽 | 巳 | 丙 | 午 | 丁 | 未 | 坤 | 申 | 庚 | 酉 | 辛 | 戌 | 乾 | 亥 |
|---|---|---|---|---|---|---|---|---|---|---|---|---|---|---|---|---|---|---|---|---|---|---|---|---|
| Clash | | | | | | | | | | | | | | | | | | | | | | | | ● |
| Killings | | ● | ● | ● | | | | | | | | | | | | | | | | | | | | |
| Direct K | | | ● | ● | | | | | | | | | | | | | | | | | | | | |
| Punish | | | | | | | | | | | | | ● | ● | | | | | | | | | | |
| Seated | | | | | | | | | | | | | ● | ● | | | | | | | | | | |
| Harm | | | | | | ● | | | | | | | | | | | | | | | | | | |
| Retreat | | | | | | | | | | | | | | | ○ | ○ | ○ | ○ | ○ | ○ | ○ | | | |
| 3-Combo | | | | | | ○ | | | | | | | | | | | | | | | | | | |
| Summons | | | | | | | | | | | | ○ | | | | | | | | | | | | |
| Grotto | | | | | | | | | | | | | | ○ | | | | | | | | | | |
| Pit | | | | | | | | | | | | | | | | | ○ | | | | | | | |
| Piercing H | | | | | | | | | | | | | | | | | | ○ | ○ | ○ | ○ | ○ | ○ | ○ |
| Free | ✓ | | | | ✓ | | ✓ | | ✓ | | ✓ | | | | | | | | | | | | | |

● major    ○ minor    ✓ taboo free

# Part-3: Personalizing the Facing (仙命宜忌)

**Year Pillar:** 癸未 (1883, 1943, 2003, 2063…)    **nà yīn element: Wood**

### Sitting Mountain

| | 壬 | 子 | 癸 | 丑 | 艮 | 寅 | 甲 | 卯 | 乙 | 辰 | 巽 | 巳 | 丙 | 午 | 丁 | 未 | 坤 | 申 | 庚 | 酉 | 辛 | 戌 | 乾 | 亥 |
|---|---|---|---|---|---|---|---|---|---|---|---|---|---|---|---|---|---|---|---|---|---|---|---|---|
| Clash | | | | ● | | | | | | | | | | | | | | | | | | | | |
| Killings | | | | | | | | | | | | | | | | | | ● | | ● | | ● | | |
| Direct K | | | | | | | | | | | | | | | | | | | | | | ● | | |
| Punish | | | | | | | | ● | | | | | | | | | | | | | | | | |
| Seated | | | | | | | | | | | | | | | | ● | | | | | | | | |
| Harm | | ● | | | | | | | | | | | | | | | | | | | | | | |
| Retreat | | | | | | | | | | ○ | | ○ | | ○ | | ○ | | | | | | | | |
| 3-Combo | | | | | | | | ○ | | | | | | | | | | | | | | | | |
| Summons | | | | | | ○ | | | | | | | | | | ○ | | | | | | | | |
| Grotto | | | | | | | | | | | | | | | | ○ | | | | | | | | |
| Pit | | | | | | | | | | | | | | | | | | ○ | | | | | | |
| Piercing H | | | | | | | | | | | | | | | | | | | | ○ | ○ | ○ | | ○ |
| Free | ✓ | ✓ | ✓ | | | | | | | | | | | | | | | | | | | | | ✓ |

● major   ○ minor   ✓ taboo free

# Part-3: Personalizing the Facing (仙命宜忌)

**Year Pillar:** 甲申 (1884, 1944, 2004, 2064…)    **nà yīn element: Water**

**Sitting Mountain**

| | 壬 | 子 | 癸 | 丑 | 艮 | 寅 | 甲 | 卯 | 乙 | 辰 | 巽 | 巳 | 丙 | 午 | 丁 | 未 | 坤 | 申 | 庚 | 酉 | 辛 | 戌 | 乾 | 亥 |
|---|---|---|---|---|---|---|---|---|---|---|---|---|---|---|---|---|---|---|---|---|---|---|---|---|
| Clash | | | | | | ● | | | | | | | | | | | | | | | | | | |
| Killings | | | | | | | | | | | | ● | ● | ● | | ● | | | | | | | | |
| Direct K | | | | | | | | | | | | ● | | | | | | | | | | | | |
| Punish | | | | | | | | | | | | | ● | | | | | | | | | | | |
| Seated | | | | | | | | | | | | | | | | | | ● | | | | | | |
| Harm | | | | | | | | | | | | | | | | | | | | | | | | ● |
| Retreat | | | | ○ | ○ | ○ | ○ | | | | | | | | | | | | | | | | | |
| 3-Combo | | ○ | | | | | | | | ○ | | | | | | | | | | | | | | |
| Summons | | | | | | | | | | | | | | | | | | | | | | | | ○ |
| Grotto | | | | | | | | | | | | | | | | | ○ | | | | | | | |
| Pit | | | | | | | | | | | | | | | | | | | | ○ | | | | |
| Piercing H | | | | | | | | | | ○ | | | | | | | | ○ | | | | ○ | | |
| Free | ✓ | | | | | | | | | | ✓ | | | | | | | | | | ✓ | ✓ | ✓ | |

● major    ○ minor    ✓ taboo free

# Part-3: Personalizing the Facing (仙命宜忌)

**Year Pillar: 乙酉** (1885, 1945, 2005, 2065…)  **nà yīn element: Water**

### Sitting Mountain

| | 壬 | 子 | 癸 | 丑 | 艮 | 寅 | 甲 | 卯 | 乙 | 辰 | 巽 | 巳 | 丙 | 午 | 丁 | 未 | 坤 | 申 | 庚 | 酉 | 辛 | 戌 | 乾 | 亥 |
|---|---|---|---|---|---|---|---|---|---|---|---|---|---|---|---|---|---|---|---|---|---|---|---|---|
| Clash | | | | | | | | ● | | | | | | | | | | | | | | | | |
| Killings | | | | | | | ● | ● | ● | ● | | | | | | | | | | | | | | |
| Direct K | | | | | | ● | | | | ● | | | | | | | | | | | | | | |
| Punish | | | | | | | | | | | | | | | | | | | | | | | | |
| Seated | | | | | | | | | | | | | ● | ● | | | | | | | | | | |
| Harm | | | | | | | | | | | | | | | | | | | | | | ● | | |
| Retreat | ○ | ○ | ○ | | | | | | | | | | | | | | | | | | | | | |
| 3-Combo | | | | ○ | | | | | | | | ○ | | | | | | | | | | | | |
| Summons | | | | | | | | | | | | | | | ○ | | | | | | | | | |
| Grotto | | | | | | | | | | | | | | | | | | ○ | | | | | | |
| Pit | | | | | | | | | | | | | | | | | | | | ○ | | | | |
| Piercing H | | | | | | | | | | | | | | | | | ○ | ○ | | | | | ○ | |
| Free | | | | | | | | | | | | | | | | | | | | ✓ | ✓ | ✓ | | |

● major   ○ minor   ✓ taboo free

# Part-3: Personalizing the Facing (仙命宜忌)

**Year Pillar:** 丙戌 (1886, 1946, 2006, 2066…)  **nà yīn element: Earth**

| | Sitting Mountain | | | | | | | | | | | | | | | | | | | | | | | |
|---|---|---|---|---|---|---|---|---|---|---|---|---|---|---|---|---|---|---|---|---|---|---|---|---|
| | 壬 | 子 | 癸 | 丑 | 艮 | 寅 | 甲 | 卯 | 乙 | 辰 | 巽 | 巳 | 丙 | 午 | 丁 | 未 | 坤 | 申 | 庚 | 酉 | 辛 | 戌 | 乾 | 亥 |
| **Clash** | | | | | | | | | | ● | | | | | | | | | | | | | | |
| **Killings** | ● | ● | ● | | | | | | | | | | | | | | | | | | | | | |
| **Direct K** | | | ● | | | | | | | | | | | | | | | | | | | | | |
| **Punish** | | | ● | | | | | | | | | | | | | | | | | | | | | |
| **Seated** | | | | | | | | | | | | | | | | | | | | | | ● | | |
| **Harm** | | | | | | | | | | | | | | | | | | | | ● | | | | |
| **Retreat** | | | | | | | | | | | | | ○ | ○ | ○ | ○ | ○ | | ○ | | | | | |
| **3-Combo** | | | | | | ○ | | | | | | | | | ○ | | | | | | | | | |
| **Summons** | | | | | | | | | | | | ○ | | | | | | | | | | | | |
| **Grotto** | | | | | | | | | | | | | | | | | | | | ○ | | | | |
| **Pit** | | | | | | | | | | | | | | | | | | | | | | | ○ | |
| **Piercing H** | | | | | | ○ | | ○ | ○ | ○ | | ○ | | | | | | | | | | | | |
| **Free** | ✓ | | | | | | | | | | | | | ✓ | | | | | | | | ✓ | | |

● major    ○ minor    ✓ taboo free

# Part-3: Personalizing the Facing (仙命宜忌)

**Year Pillar:** 丁亥 (1887, 1947, 2007, 2067…)

**nà yīn element:** Earth

### Sitting Mountain

| | 壬 | 子 | 癸 | 丑 | 艮 | 寅 | 甲 | 卯 | 乙 | 辰 | 巽 | 巳 | 丙 | 午 | 丁 | 未 | 坤 | 申 | 庚 | 酉 | 辛 | 戌 | 乾 | 亥 |
|---|---|---|---|---|---|---|---|---|---|---|---|---|---|---|---|---|---|---|---|---|---|---|---|---|
| Clash | | | | | | | | | | | | ● | | | | | | | | | | | | |
| Killings | | | | | | | | | | | | | | | | | | ● | | ● | ● | ● | | |
| Direct K | | | | | | | | | | | | | | | | | | | | | | ● | | |
| Punish | | | | | | | | | | | | | | | | | | | | | | | ● | ● |
| Seated | | | | | | | | | | | | | | | | | | | | | | | | |
| Harm | | | | | | | | | | | | | | | ● | | | | | | | | | |
| Retreat | | | | | | | | | | ○ | ○ | ○ | ○ | ○ | | | | | | | | | | |
| 3-Combo | | | | | | | | ○ | | | | | | | ○ | | | | | | | | | |
| Summons | | | | | | ○ | | | | | | | | | | | | | | | | | | |
| Grotto | | | | | | | | | | | | | | | | | | | | | ○ | | | |
| Pit | ○ | | | | | | | | | | | | | | | | | | | | | | | |
| Piercing H | | | | | | | | ○ | ○ | ○ | | | | | | | | | | | | | | |
| Free | ✓ | ✓ | ✓ | | | | | | | | | | | | | | | | | | ✓ | | | |

● major    ○ minor    ✓ taboo free

# Part-3: Personalizing the Facing (仙命宜忌)

Year Pillar: 戊子 (1888, 1948, 2008, 2068…)    nà yīn element: Fire

**Sitting Mountain**

| | 壬 | 子 | 癸 | 丑 | 艮 | 寅 | 甲 | 卯 | 乙 | 辰 | 巽 | 巳 | 丙 | 午 | 丁 | 未 | 坤 | 申 | 庚 | 酉 | 辛 | 戌 | 乾 | 亥 |
|---|---|---|---|---|---|---|---|---|---|---|---|---|---|---|---|---|---|---|---|---|---|---|---|---|
| **Clash** | | | | | | | | | | | | | | ● | | | | | | | | | | |
| **Killings** | | | | | | | | | | | | | ● | ● | ● | | | | | | | | | |
| **Direct K** | | | | | | | | | | | | ● | | | | | | | | | | | | |
| **Punish** | | | | | | | | ● | | | | | | | | | | | | | | | | |
| **Seated** | | ● | | | | | | | | | | | | | | | | | | | | | | |
| **Harm** | | | | | | | | | | | | | | | | ● | | | | | | | | |
| **Retreat** | | | | ○ | ○ | ○ | ○ | ○ | | | | | | | | | | | | | | | | |
| **3-Combo** | | | | | | | | | | | | | | | | | ○ | | | | | | | |
| **Summons** | | | | | | | | | | | | | | | | | | | | | ○ | | ○ | |
| **Grotto** | ○ | | | | | | | | | | | | | | | | | | | | | | | |
| **Pit** | | | ○ | | | | | | | | | | | | | | | | | | | | | |
| **Piercing H** | ○ | ○ | ○ | | | | | | | | | | | | | | | | | | | | | |
| **Free** | | | | | | | | | | ✓ | | | | | | | | ✓ | ✓ | ✓ | ✓ | ✓ | ✓ | ✓ |

● major    ○ minor    ✓ taboo free

# Part-3: Personalizing the Facing (仙命宜忌)

**Year Pillar:** 己丑 (1889, 1949, 2009, 2069…)  
**nà yīn element:** Fire

### Sitting Mountain

| | 壬 | 子 | 癸 | 丑 | 艮 | 寅 | 甲 | 卯 | 乙 | 辰 | 巽 | 巳 | 丙 | 午 | 丁 | 未 | 坤 | 申 | 庚 | 酉 | 辛 | 戌 | 乾 | 亥 |
|---|---|---|---|---|---|---|---|---|---|---|---|---|---|---|---|---|---|---|---|---|---|---|---|---|
| Clash | | | | | | | | | | | | | | | | ● | | | | | | | | |
| Killings | | | | ● | | ● | | ● | | ● | | | | | | | | | | | | | | |
| Direct K | | | | | | | | | | ● | | | | | | | | | | | | | | |
| Punish | | | | | | | | | | | | | | | | | | | | | | ● | | |
| Seated | | | | ● | | | | | | | | | | | | | | | | | | | | |
| Harm | | | | | | | | | | | | | | ● | | | | | | | | | | |
| Retreat | ○ | ○ | ○ | | | | | | | | | | | | | | | | | | | | | |
| 3-Combo | | | | | | | | | | | | ○ | | | | | | | | ○ | | | | |
| Summons | | | | | | | | | | | | | | | | | | ○ | | | | | | |
| Grotto | | ○ | | | | | | | | | | | | | | | | | | | | | | |
| Pit | | | | | | | | ○ | | | | | | | | | | | | | | | | |
| Piercing H | ○ | ○ | ○ | | | | | | | | | | | | | | | | | | | | | |
| Free | | | | | | | | | | ✓ | | ✓ | | ✓ | | ✓ | | | | ✓ | | | | ✓ |

● major    ○ minor    ✓ taboo free

The yīn House Handbook

# Part-3: Personalizing the Facing (仙命宜忌)

**Year Pillar: 庚寅 (1890, 1950, 2010, 2070…)**  
**nà yīn element: Wood**

### Sitting Mountain

| | 壬 | 子 | 癸 | 丑 | 艮 | 寅 | 甲 | 卯 | 乙 | 辰 | 巽 | 巳 | 丙 | 午 | 丁 | 未 | 坤 | 申 | 庚 | 酉 | 辛 | 戌 | 乾 | 亥 |
|---|---|---|---|---|---|---|---|---|---|---|---|---|---|---|---|---|---|---|---|---|---|---|---|---|
| Clash | | | | | | | | | | | | | | | | | | • | | | | | | |
| Killings | | • | • | • | | | | | | | | | | | | | | | | | | | | |
| Direct K | | • | | | | | | | | | | | | | | | | | | | | | | |
| Punish | | | | | | | | | | | | • | | | | | | | | | | | | |
| Seated | | | | | | • | | | | | | | | | | | | | | | | | | |
| Harm | | | | | | | | | | | | • | | | | | | | | | | | | |
| Retreat | | | | | | | | | | | | | | | | ○ | ○ | ○ | ○ | | | | | |
| 3-Combo | | | | | | | | | | | | | | ○ | | | | | | | | | | |
| Summons | | | | | | | | | | | | ○ | | | | | | | | | | ○ | | |
| Grotto | | | | | | | | | ○ | | | | | | | | | | | | | | | |
| Pit | | | | | | | | ○ | | | | | | | | | | | | | | | | |
| Piercing H | | | | | | | | | | | | | | | | | | ○ | ○ | ○ | ○ | ○ | ○ | |
| Free | | | | | | | | | | ✓ | ✓ | | ✓ | | ✓ | | ✓ | | | | | | | |

● major   ○ minor   ✓ taboo free

# Part-3: Personalizing the Facing (仙命宜忌)

**Year Pillar:** 辛卯 (1891, 1951, 2011, 2071…)  **nà yīn element:** Wood

**Sitting Mountain**

| | 壬 | 子 | 癸 | 丑 | 艮 | 寅 | 甲 | 卯 | 乙 | 辰 | 巽 | 巳 | 丙 | 午 | 丁 | 未 | 坤 | 申 | 庚 | 酉 | 辛 | 戌 | 乾 | 亥 |
|---|---|---|---|---|---|---|---|---|---|---|---|---|---|---|---|---|---|---|---|---|---|---|---|---|
| Clash | | | | | | | | | | | | | | | | | | | | | | | | |
| Killings | | | | | | | | | | | | | | | | | | ● | | ● | | ● | | |
| Direct K | | | | | | | | | | | | | | | | | | | | ● | | ● | | |
| Punish | | ● | | | | | | | | | | | | | | | | | | | | | | |
| Seated | | | | | | | | ● | | | | | | | | | | | | | | | | |
| Harm | | | | | | | | | | ● | | | | | | | | | | | | | | |
| Retreat | | | | | | | | | | ○ | ○ | ○ | ○ | ○ | | | | | | | | | | |
| 3-Combo | | | | | | | | | | | | | | | | ○ | | | | | | | | |
| Summons | | | | | | ○ | | | | | | | | | | | | | | | | | | |
| Grotto | | | | | | | | ○ | | | | | | | | | | | | | | | | |
| Pit | | | | | | | | | | | | ○ | | | | | | | | | | | | |
| Piercing H | | | | | | | | | | | | | | | | | | ○ | ○ | ○ | ○ | ○ | ○ | |
| Free | ✓ | ✓ | ✓ | | | | | | | | | | | | | | | | | | ✓ | | | |

● major   ○ minor   ✓ taboo free

# Part-3: Personalizing the Facing (仙命宜忌)

**Year Pillar:** 壬辰 (1892, 1952, 2012, 2072....)    **nà yīn element:** Water

### Sitting Mountain

| | 壬 | 子 | 癸 | 丑 | 艮 | 寅 | 甲 | 卯 | 乙 | 辰 | 巽 | 巳 | 丙 | 午 | 丁 | 未 | 坤 | 申 | 庚 | 酉 | 辛 | 戌 | 乾 | 亥 |
|---|---|---|---|---|---|---|---|---|---|---|---|---|---|---|---|---|---|---|---|---|---|---|---|---|
| Clash | | | | | | | | | | | | | | | | | | | | | | ● | | |
| Killings | | | | | | | | | | | | ● | ● | ● | ● | | | | | | | | | |
| Direct K | | | | | | | | | | | | | ● | | | | | | | | | | | |
| Punish | | | | | | | | | | ● | | | | | | | | | | | | | | |
| Seated | | | | | | | | | | ● | | | | | | | | | | | | | | |
| Harm | | | | | | | | ● | | | | | | | | | | | | | | | | |
| Retreat | ○ | ○ | ○ | ○ | ○ | | | | | | | | | | | | | | | | | | | |
| 3-Combo | ○ | | | | | | | | | | | | | | | | | | | | | | | |
| Summons | | | | | | | | | | | | | | | | | | ○ | | | | | ○ | |
| Grotto | | | | | | | | | | ○ | | ○ | | | | | | | | | | | | |
| Pit | | | | | | | | | | | | ○ | | | | | | | | | | | | |
| Piercing H | | ○ | ○ | | | | | | | | | | | | | ○ | | | ○ | | | ○ | | |
| Free | ✓ | ✓ | | | | | | | | | | | | | | | | | ✓ | ✓ | ✓ | | | ✓ |

● major    ○ minor    ✓ taboo free

# Part-3: Personalizing the Facing (仙命宜忌)

**Year Pillar:** 癸巳 (1893, 1953, 2013, 2073…)   **nà yīn element:** Water

**Sitting Mountain**

| | 壬 | 子 | 癸 | 丑 | 艮 | 寅 | 甲 | 卯 | 乙 | 辰 | 巽 | 巳 | 丙 | 午 | 丁 | 未 | 坤 | 申 | 庚 | 酉 | 辛 | 戌 | 乾 | 亥 |
|---|---|---|---|---|---|---|---|---|---|---|---|---|---|---|---|---|---|---|---|---|---|---|---|---|
| Clash | | | | | | | | | | | | | | | | | | | | | | | | ● |
| Killings | | | | | | | ● | ● | ● | ● | | | | | | | | | | | | | | |
| Direct K | | | | | | | | ● | | | | | | | | | | | | | | | | |
| Punish | | | | | | ● | | | | | | | | | | | | | | | | | | |
| Seated | | | | | | | | | | | | | | ● | | | | | | | | | | |
| Harm | | | | | | ● | | | | | | | | | | | | | | | | | | |
| Retreat | ○ | ○ | ○ | | | | | | | | | | | | | | | | | | | | | |
| 3-Combo | | | | ○ | | | | | | | | | | | | | | | | | | | | |
| Summons | | | | | | | | | | | | | | | | | | | | | | | | |
| Grotto | | | | | | | | | | | | ○ | | | | | | | | | | | | |
| Pit | | | | | | | | | | | | | ○ | | | | | | | | | | | |
| Piercing H | | | | ○ | | | | | | ○ | | | | | | ○ | | ○ | | | | | | |
| Free | | | | | | | | | | | | | | | | ✓ | | ✓ | | | | ✓ | | ✓ |

● major   ○ minor   ✓ taboo free

*The yīn House Handbook*

# Part-3: Personalizing the Facing (仙命宜忌)

**Year Pillar:** 甲午 (1894, 1954, 2014, 2074…)  
**nà yīn element:** Metal

### Sitting Mountain

| | 壬 | 子 | 癸 | 丑 | 艮 | 寅 | 甲 | 卯 | 乙 | 辰 | 巽 | 巳 | 丙 | 午 | 丁 | 未 | 坤 | 申 | 庚 | 酉 | 辛 | 戌 | 乾 | 亥 |
|---|---|---|---|---|---|---|---|---|---|---|---|---|---|---|---|---|---|---|---|---|---|---|---|---|
| Clash     |   | ● |   |   |   |   |   |   |   |   |   |   |   |   |   |   |   |   |   |   |   |   |   |   |
| Killings  | ● | ● | ● |   |   |   |   |   |   |   |   |   |   |   |   |   |   |   |   |   |   |   |   |   |
| Direct K  |   |   | ● |   |   |   |   |   |   |   |   |   |   |   |   |   |   |   |   |   |   |   |   |   |
| Punish    |   |   |   |   |   |   |   |   |   |   |   |   | ● | ● |   |   |   |   |   |   |   |   |   |   |
| Seated    |   |   |   |   |   |   |   |   |   |   |   |   |   | ● |   |   |   |   |   |   |   |   |   |   |
| Harm      |   |   |   |   |   |   |   |   |   |   |   |   |   |   |   | ● |   |   |   |   |   |   |   |   |
| Retreat   |   |   |   |   |   |   |   |   |   |   |   |   |   |   |   |   | ○ | ○ | ○ | ○ | ○ |   | ○ |   |
| 3-Combo   |   |   |   |   |   |   |   |   |   |   | ○ |   |   |   |   |   |   |   |   |   |   |   |   |   |
| Summons   |   |   |   |   |   |   |   |   |   |   |   |   | ○ |   |   |   |   |   |   |   |   |   |   |   |
| Grotto    |   |   |   |   |   |   |   |   |   |   |   |   |   | ○ |   |   |   |   |   |   |   |   |   |   |
| Pit       |   |   |   |   |   |   |   |   |   |   |   |   | ○ | ○ | ○ | ○ |   |   |   |   |   |   |   |   |
| Piercing H|   |   |   |   |   |   |   |   |   |   |   |   | ○ | ○ | ○ | ○ |   |   |   |   |   |   |   |   |
| Free      | ✓ | ✓ | ✓ | ✓ | ✓ | ✓ |   |   |   |   |   |   |   |   |   |   |   |   |   |   |   |   | ✓ |   |

● major   ○ minor   ✓ taboo free

# Part-3: Personalizing the Facing (仙命宜忌)

**Year Pillar: 乙未 (1895, 1955, 2015, 2075…)**  
**nà yīn element: Metal**

### Sitting Mountain

| | 壬 | 子 | 癸 | 丑 | 艮 | 寅 | 甲 | 卯 | 乙 | 辰 | 巽 | 巳 | 丙 | 午 | 丁 | 未 | 坤 | 申 | 庚 | 酉 | 辛 | 戌 | 乾 | 亥 |
|---|---|---|---|---|---|---|---|---|---|---|---|---|---|---|---|---|---|---|---|---|---|---|---|---|
| Clash | | | | ● | | | | | | | | | | | | | | | | | | | | |
| Killings | | | | | | | | | | | | | | | | | | | ● | ● | ● | | | |
| Direct K | | | | | | | | | | | | | | | | | | | | | | ● | | |
| Punish | | | | | | ● | | | | | | | | | | | | | | | | | | |
| Seated | | | | | | | | | | | | | | | | ● | | | | | | | | |
| Harm | | ● | | | | | | | | | | | | | | | | | | | | | | |
| Retreat | | | | | | | | | | ○ | ○ | ○ | ○ | | | | | | | | | | | |
| 3-Combo | | | | | | | | ○ | | | | | | | | | | | | | | | | |
| Summons | | | | | | ○ | | | | | | | | | | | | | | | | | | |
| Grotto | | | | | | | | | | | | | | | ○ | | | | | | | | | |
| Pit | | | | | | | | | | | | | | | | ○ | | | | | | | | |
| Piercing H | | | | | | | | | | | | | ○ | ○ | ○ | | | | | | | | | |
| Free | ✓ | ✓ | ✓ | | | | | | | | | | | | | | | | | | | | | ✓ |

● major   ○ minor   ✓ taboo free

# Part-3: Personalizing the Facing (仙命宜忌)

Year Pillar: 丙申 (1896, 1956, 2016, 2076…)  nà yīn element: Fire

**Sitting Mountain**

| | 壬 | 子 | 癸 | 丑 | 艮 | 寅 | 甲 | 卯 | 乙 | 辰 | 巽 | 巳 | 丙 | 午 | 丁 | 未 | 坤 | 申 | 庚 | 酉 | 辛 | 戌 | 乾 | 亥 |
|---|---|---|---|---|---|---|---|---|---|---|---|---|---|---|---|---|---|---|---|---|---|---|---|---|
| Clash | | | | | | ● | | | | | | | | | | | | | | | | | | |
| Killings | | | | | | | | | | | | | ● | ● | ● | | | | | | | | | |
| Direct K | | | | | | | | | | | | | | | ● | ● | | | | | | | | |
| Punish | | | | | | | | | | | | ● | | | ● | | | | | | | | | |
| Seated | | | | | | | | | | | | | | | | | | ● | | | | | | |
| Harm | | | | | | | | | | | | | | | | | | | | | | | | ● |
| Retreat | | | ○ | ○ | ○ | ○ | ○ | ○ | | | | | | | | | | | | | | | | |
| 3-Combo | ○ | | | | | | | | | | | ○ | | | | | | | | | | | | |
| Summons | | | | | | | | | | | | | | | | | | | | | | | ○ | |
| Grotto | | | | | | | | | | | | | | | | | | | ○ | | | | | |
| Pit | | | | | | | | | | | | | | | | | | | | | ○ | | | |
| Piercing H | ○ | ○ | ○ | | | | | | | | | | | | | | | | | | | | | |
| Free | | | | | | | | | | | ✓ | | | | | | | | | | ✓ | ✓ | ✓ | ✓ |

● major    ○ minor    ✓ taboo free

# Part-3: Personalizing the Facing (仙命宜忌)

**Year Pillar: 丁酉** (1897, 1957, 2017, 2077…)  nà yīn element: Fire

Sitting Mountain

| | 壬 | 子 | 癸 | 丑 | 艮 | 寅 | 甲 | 卯 | 乙 | 辰 | 巽 | 巳 | 丙 | 午 | 丁 | 未 | 坤 | 申 | 庚 | 酉 | 辛 | 戌 | 乾 | 亥 |
|---|---|---|---|---|---|---|---|---|---|---|---|---|---|---|---|---|---|---|---|---|---|---|---|---|
| Clash | | | | | | | | ● | | | | | | | | | | | | | | | | |
| Killings | | | | | | ● | | ● | | ● | | | | | | | | | | | | | | |
| Direct K | | | | | | | | | | ● | | | | | | | | | | | | | | |
| Punish | | | | | | | | | | | | | | | | | | | | | | ● | | |
| Seated | | | | | | | | | | | | | | | | | | | ● | ● | | | | |
| Harm | | | | | | | | | | | | | | | | | | | | | | | | |
| Retreat | ○ | ○ | ○ | | | | | | | | | | | | | | | | | | | | | |
| 3-Combo | | | | | ○ | | | | | | | | | | | | | | | | | | | |
| Summons | | | | | | | | | | | | | ○ | | | | | | | | | | | |
| Grotto | | | | | | | | | | | | | | | | | | ○ | | ○ | | | | |
| Pit | | | | | | | | | | | | | | | | | | | | | ○ | | | |
| Piercing H | ○ | ○ | ○ | | | | | | | | | | | | | | | | | | | ○ | | ○ |
| Free | | | | | | | | | | | | ✓ | | ✓ | ✓ | ✓ | ✓ | | | | | | | |

● major   ○ minor   ✓ taboo free

# Part-3: Personalizing the Facing (仙命宜忌)

**Year Pillar:** 戊戌 (1898, 1958, 2018, 2078…)    **nà yīn element:** Wood

### Sitting Mountain

| | 壬 | 子 | 癸 | 丑 | 艮 | 寅 | 甲 | 卯 | 乙 | 辰 | 巽 | 巳 | 丙 | 午 | 丁 | 未 | 坤 | 申 | 庚 | 酉 | 辛 | 戌 | 乾 | 亥 |
|---|---|---|---|---|---|---|---|---|---|---|---|---|---|---|---|---|---|---|---|---|---|---|---|---|
| **Clash** | | | | | | | | | | ● | | | | | | | | | | | | | | |
| **Killings** | ● | ● | ● | ● | | | | | | | | | | | | | | | | | | | | |
| **Direct K** | | | ● | | | | | | | | | | | | | | | | | | | | | |
| **Punish** | | | | ● | | | | | | | | | | | | | | | | | | | | |
| **Seated** | | | | | | | | | | | | | | | | | | | | | | ● | | |
| **Harm** | | | | | | | | | | | | | | | | | | | | ● | | | | |
| **Retreat** | | | | | | | ○ | ○ | ○ | ○ | | | | | | | | | ○ | | ○ | ○ | | |
| **3-Combo** | | | | | | | | | | | | | | ○ | | | | | | | | | | |
| **Summons** | | | | | | | | | | | | ○ | | | | | | | | | | | | |
| **Grotto** | | | | | | | | | | | | | | | | | | | | | ○ | | | |
| **Pit** | | | | | | | | | | | | | | | | | | | | | ○ | | ○ | ○ |
| **Piercing H** | | | | | | | | | | | | | | | | | | | | ○ | ○ | ○ | ○ | ○ |
| **Free** | ✓ | | | | | ✓ | ✓ | ✓ | ✓ | | ✓ | | | | | | | ✓ | | | | | | |

● major    ○ minor    ✓ taboo free

# Part-3: Personalizing the Facing (仙命宜忌)

**Year Pillar: 己亥 (1899, 1959, 2019, 2079…)**

**nà yīn element: Wood**

## Sitting Mountain

| | 壬 | 子 | 癸 | 丑 | 艮 | 寅 | 甲 | 卯 | 乙 | 辰 | 巽 | 巳 | 丙 | 午 | 丁 | 未 | 坤 | 申 | 庚 | 酉 | 辛 | 戌 | 乾 | 亥 |
|---|---|---|---|---|---|---|---|---|---|---|---|---|---|---|---|---|---|---|---|---|---|---|---|---|
| Clash | | | | | | | | | | | | ● | | | | | | | | | | | | |
| Killings | | | | | | | | | | | | | | | | | | ● | | ● | | ● | | |
| Direct K | | | | | | | | | | | | | | | | | | | | | | ● | | |
| Punish | | | | | | | | | | | | | | | ● | ● | | | | | | | | |
| Seated | | | | | | | | | | | | | | | | | | | | | | | | ● |
| Harm | | | | | | | | | | | | | | | | | | ● | | | | | | |
| Retreat | | | | | | | | | | ○ | ○ | ○ | ○ | ○ | | | | | | | | | | |
| 3-Combo | | | | | | | ○ | | | | | | | | | ○ | | | | | | | | ○ |
| Summons | | | | | | ○ | | | | | | | | | | | | | | | | | | |
| Grotto | | | | | | | | | | | | | | | | | | | | ○ | | | ○ | |
| Pit | ○ | | | | | | | | | | | | | | | | | | | | | | | |
| Piercing H | | | | | | | | | | | | | | | | | | | ○ | ○ | ○ | ○ | ○ | |
| Free | ✓ | ✓ | ✓ | | | | | | | | | | | | | | | | | | | | | |

● major  ○ minor  ✓ taboo free

# Part-3: Personalizing the Facing (仙命宜忌)

**Year Pillar: 庚子 (1900, 1960, 2020, 2080…)   nà yīn element: Earth**

**Sitting Mountain**

| | 壬 | 子 | 癸 | 丑 | 艮 | 寅 | 甲 | 卯 | 乙 | 辰 | 巽 | 巳 | 丙 | 午 | 丁 | 未 | 坤 | 申 | 庚 | 酉 | 辛 | 戌 | 乾 | 亥 |
|---|---|---|---|---|---|---|---|---|---|---|---|---|---|---|---|---|---|---|---|---|---|---|---|---|
| Clash | | | | | | | | | | | | | | ● | | | | | | | | | | |
| Killings | | | | | | | | | | | | ● | ● | ● | ● | | | | | | | | |
| Direct K | | | | | | | | | | | | | | | ● | | | | | | | | | |
| Punish | | | | | | | | ● | | | | | | | | | | | | | | | | |
| Seated | | | | | | | | | | | | | | | | | | | | | | | | |
| Harm | | | | | | | | | | | | | | | | ● | | | | | | | | |
| Retreat | | ○ | ○ | ○ | ○ | ○ | | | | | | | | | | | | | | | | | | |
| 3-Combo | | | | | | | | | | ○ | | | | | | | | | | | | | | |
| Summons | | | | | | | | | | | | | | | | | | | ○ | | | | | |
| Grotto | ○ | | | | | | | | | | | | | | | | | | | | | | | |
| Pit | | | | | | | ○ | | | | | | | | | | | | | | | | | |
| Piercing H | | | | | | | | | ○ | ○ | ○ | ○ | | | | | | | | | | | | |

| | | |
|---|---|---|
| Free | ✓ | ✓ ✓ ✓ ✓ ✓ |

● major   ○ minor   ✓ taboo free

104   The yīn House Handbook

# Part-3: Personalizing the Facing (仙命宜忌)

**Year Pillar:** 辛丑 (1901, 1961, 2021, 2081…)    **nà yīn element:** Earth

**Sitting Mountain**

| | 壬 | 子 | 癸 | 丑 | 艮 | 寅 | 甲 | 卯 | 乙 | 辰 | 巽 | 巳 | 丙 | 午 | 丁 | 未 | 坤 | 申 | 庚 | 酉 | 辛 | 戌 | 乾 | 亥 |
|---|---|---|---|---|---|---|---|---|---|---|---|---|---|---|---|---|---|---|---|---|---|---|---|---|
| **Clash** | | | | | | | | | | | | | | | | ● | | | | | | | | |
| **Killings** | | | | | | ● | ● | ● | ● | | | | | | | | | | | | | | | |
| **Direct K** | | | | | | | | | | ● | | | | | | | | | | | | | | |
| **Punish** | | | | | | | | | | | | | | | | | | | | | | ● | | |
| **Seated** | | | | ● | | | | | | | | | | | | | | | | | | | | |
| **Harm** | | | | | | | | | | | | | | ● | | | | | | | | | | |
| **Retreat** | ○ | ○ | ○ | | | | | | | | | | | | | | | | | | | | ○ | ○ |
| **3-Combo** | | | | | | | | | | | | | ○ | | | | | | | ○ | | | | |
| **Summons** | | | | | | | | | | | | | | | | | | ○ | | | | | | |
| **Grotto** | | | | | ○ | | | | | | | | | | | | | | | | | | | |
| **Pit** | | | | | | | | | | | | ○ | | | | | | | | | | | | |
| **Piercing H** | | | | | | | ○ | ○ | ○ | ○ | | | | | | | | | | | | | | |
| **Free** | | | | | | | | | | | | | ✓ | | | ✓ | | ✓ | ✓ | | ✓ | | | |

● major    ○ minor    ✓ taboo free

# Part-3: Personalizing the Facing (仙命宜忌)

**Year Pillar: 壬寅 (1902, 1962, 2022, 2082…)**    **nà yīn element: Metal**

**Sitting Mountain**

| | 壬 | 子 | 癸 | 丑 | 艮 | 寅 | 甲 | 卯 | 乙 | 辰 | 巽 | 巳 | 丙 | 午 | 丁 | 未 | 坤 | 申 | 庚 | 酉 | 辛 | 戌 | 乾 | 亥 |
|---|---|---|---|---|---|---|---|---|---|---|---|---|---|---|---|---|---|---|---|---|---|---|---|---|
| **Clash** | | | | | | | | | | | | | | | | | ● | | | | | | | |
| **Killings** | ● | ● | ● | ● | | | | | | | | | | | | | | | | | | | | |
| **Direct K** | | | | ● | | | | | | | | | | | | | | | | | | | | |
| **Punish** | | | | | | | | | | | | ● | | | | | | | | | | | | |
| **Seated** | | | | | | ● | | | | | | | | | | | | | | | | | | |
| **Harm** | | | | | | | | | | | | | | ● | | | | | | | | | | |
| **Retreat** | | | | | | | | | | | | | | | | | | ○ | ○ | ○ | ○ | | | |
| **3-Combo** | | | | | | | | | | | | | | ○ | | | | | | | | ○ | | |
| **Summons** | | | | | | | | | | | | ○ | | | | | | | | | | | | |
| **Grotto** | | | | | | | | | | ○ | | | | | | | | | | | | | | |
| **Pit** | | | | | | | ○ | | | | | | | | | | | | | | | | | |
| **Piercing H** | | | | | | | | | | | | ○ | | ○ | ○ | ○ | | | | | | | | |

| | Free |
|---|---|
| | ✓ ✓ ✓ ✓ ✓ |

● major    ○ minor    ✓ taboo free

# Part-3: Personalizing the Facing (仙命宜忌)

**Year Pillar: 癸卯 (1903, 1963, 2023, 2083…)**  nà yīn element: Metal

### Sitting Mountain

| | 壬 | 子 | 癸 | 丑 | 艮 | 寅 | 甲 | 卯 | 乙 | 辰 | 巽 | 巳 | 丙 | 午 | 丁 | 未 | 坤 | 申 | 庚 | 酉 | 辛 | 戌 | 乾 | 亥 |
|---|---|---|---|---|---|---|---|---|---|---|---|---|---|---|---|---|---|---|---|---|---|---|---|---|
| Clash | | | | | | | | | | | | | | | | | | | | ● | | | | |
| Killings | | | | | | | | | | | | | | | | | | ● | | ● | ● | ● | | |
| Direct K | | | | | | | | | | | | | | | | | | | | | | ● | | |
| Punish | | ● | | | | | | | | | | | | | | | | | | | | | | |
| Seated | | | | | | | | ● | | | | | | | | | | | | | | | | |
| Harm | | | | | | | | | | ● | | | | | | | | | | | | | | |
| Retreat | | | | | | | | | | ○ | ○ | ○ | ○ | | | | | | | | | | | |
| 3-Combo | | | | | | | | | | | | | | | | ○ | | | | | | | | |
| Summons | | | | | | ○ | | | | | | | | | | | | | | | | | | |
| Grotto | | | | | | | | ○ | | | | | | | | | | | | | | | | |
| Pit | | | | | | | | | | ○ | | | | | | | | | | | | | | |
| Piercing H | | | | | | | | | | | | ○ | ○ | ○ | ○ | | | | | | | | | |
| Free | ✓ | ✓ | ✓ | | | | | | | | | | | | | | | | | | | ✓ | ✓ | ✓ |

● major    ○ minor    ✓ taboo free

# Part-3: Personalizing the Facing (仙命宜忌)

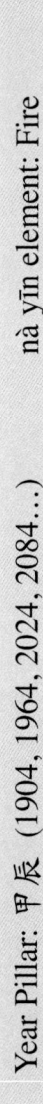

**Year Pillar:** 甲辰 (1904, 1964, 2024, 2084…)

**nà yīn element: Fire**

### Sitting Mountain

| | 壬 | 子 | 癸 | 丑 | 艮 | 寅 | 甲 | 卯 | 乙 | 辰 | 巽 | 巳 | 丙 | 午 | 丁 | 未 | 坤 | 申 | 庚 | 酉 | 辛 | 戌 | 乾 | 亥 |
|---|---|---|---|---|---|---|---|---|---|---|---|---|---|---|---|---|---|---|---|---|---|---|---|---|
| **Clash** | | | | | | | | | | | | | | | | | | | | | | ● | | |
| **Killings** | | | | | | | | | | | | ● | ● | ● | ● | | | | | | | | | |
| **Direct K** | | | | | | | | | | | | | ● | | | | | | | | | | | |
| **Punish** | | | | | | | | | ● | | | | | | | | | | | | | | | |
| **Seated** | | | | | | | | | ● | | | | | | | | | | | | | | | |
| **Harm** | | | | | | | | ● | | | | | | | | | | | | | | | | |
| **Retreat** | | | | ○ | ○ | ○ | ○ | ○ | | | | | | | | | | | | | | | | |
| **3-Combo** | | | | | | | | | | | | | | | | | | | ○ | | | | | |
| **Summons** | | | | | | | | | | | | | | | | | | | | | | | | ○ |
| **Grotto** | | | | | | | | | | | | | | | ○ | | | | | | | | | |
| **Pit** | | | | | | | | | | | ○ | | | | | | | | | | | | | |
| **Piercing H** | ○ | ○ | ○ | | | | | | | | | | | | | | | | | | | | | ○ |
| **Free** | | | | | | | | | | | | | | | | | ✓ | ✓ | ✓ | ✓ | ✓ | | | |

● major   ○ minor   ✓ taboo free

# Part-3: Personalizing the Facing (仙命宜忌)

**Year Pillar: 乙巳 (1905, 1965, 2025, 2085…)**

**nà yīn element: Fire**

### Sitting Mountain

| | 壬 | 子 | 癸 | 丑 | 艮 | 寅 | 甲 | 卯 | 乙 | 辰 | 巽 | 巳 | 丙 | 午 | 丁 | 未 | 坤 | 申 | 庚 | 酉 | 辛 | 戌 | 乾 | 亥 |
|---|---|---|---|---|---|---|---|---|---|---|---|---|---|---|---|---|---|---|---|---|---|---|---|---|
| Clash | | | | | | | | | | | | | | | | | | | | | | | | ● |
| Killings | | | | | | ● | ● | ● | ● | ● | | | | | | | | | | | | | | |
| Direct K | | | | | | | | | | ● | | | | | | | | | | | | | | |
| Punish | | | | | | ● | | | | | | | | | | ● | | | | | | | | |
| Seated | | | | | | | | | | | | ● | | | | | | | | | | | | |
| Harm | | | | | | ● | | | | | | | | | | | | | | | | | | |
| Retreat | ○ | ○ | ○ | | | | | | | | | | | | | | | | | | | ○ | ○ | ○ |
| 3-Combo | | | | ○ | | | | | | | | | | | | | | | | | | | | |
| Summons | | | | | | | | | | | | | | | | | | | | ○ | | | | |
| Grotto | | | | | | | | | | | | | | | ○ | | | ○ | | | | | | |
| Pit | | | | | | | | | | | | | | ○ | | | | | | | | | | |
| Piercing H | ○ | ○ | ○ | | | | | | | | | | | | | | | | | | | | | |
| Free | | | | ✓ | | | | | | | | | | | | ✓ | ✓ | ✓ | ✓ | | ✓ | | | |

● major  ○ minor  ✓ taboo free

陰宅手冊

The yīn House Handbook

# Part-3: Personalizing the Facing (仙命宜忌)

Year Pillar: 丙午 (1906, 1966, 2026, 2086…)  
nà yīn element: Water

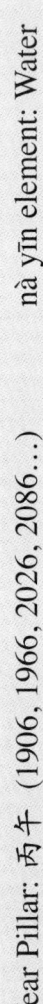

**Sitting Mountain**

| | 壬 | 子 | 癸 | 丑 | 艮 | 寅 | 甲 | 卯 | 乙 | 辰 | 巽 | 巳 | 丙 | 午 | 丁 | 未 | 坤 | 申 | 庚 | 酉 | 辛 | 戌 | 乾 | 亥 |
|---|---|---|---|---|---|---|---|---|---|---|---|---|---|---|---|---|---|---|---|---|---|---|---|---|
| **Clash** | ● | | | | | | | | | | | | | | | | | | | | | | | |
| **Killings** | ● | ● | ● | | | | | | | | | | | | | | | | | | | | | |
| **Direct K** | | | ● | ● | | | | | | | | | | | | | | | | | | | | |
| **Punish** | | | | | | | | | | | | | ● | | | | | | | | | | | |
| **Seated** | | | | | | | | | | | | | | ● | | | | | | | | | | |
| **Harm** | | | | ● | | | | | | | | | | | | | | | | | | | | |
| **Retreat** | | | | | | | | | | | | ○ | ○ | ○ | ○ | ○ | | | | | | | | |
| **3-Combo** | | | | | | ○ | | | | | | | | | | | | | | | | | | |
| **Summons** | | | | | | | | | | | | ○ | | | | | | | | | | | | |
| **Grotto** | | | | | | | | | | | | | | ○ | | | | | | | | | | |
| **Pit** | | | | | | | | | | | | | | | ○ | | | | | | | | | |
| **Piercing H** | | | | | | | | | | ○ | | | | | | | ○ | | | | | ○ | | |
| **Free** | | | | | | | | | ✓ | | ✓ | ✓ | | | | | | | | | | | | ✓ |

● major    ○ minor    ✓ taboo free

# Part-3: Personalizing the Facing (仙命宜忌)

**Year Pillar:** 丁未 (1907, 1967, 2027, 2087…)

**nà yīn element:** Water

**Sitting Mountain**

| | 壬 | 子 | 癸 | 丑 | 艮 | 寅 | 甲 | 卯 | 乙 | 辰 | 巽 | 巳 | 丙 | 午 | 丁 | 未 | 坤 | 申 | 庚 | 酉 | 辛 | 戌 | 乾 | 亥 |
|---|---|---|---|---|---|---|---|---|---|---|---|---|---|---|---|---|---|---|---|---|---|---|---|---|
| Clash | | | | ● | | | | | | | | | | | | | | | | | | | | |
| Killings | | | | | | | | | | | | | | | ● | ● | ● | ● | ● | | | | | |
| Direct K | | | | | | | | | | | | | | | | | | | | | | ● | ● | |
| Punish | | | | | | | ● | | | | | | | | | | | | | | | | | |
| Seated | | | | | | | | | | | | | | | ● | | | | | | | | | |
| Harm | | | | | | | | | | | ● | | | | | | | | | | | | | |
| Retreat | | | | | | | | | | ○ | ○ | ○ | ○ | ○ | | | | | | | | | | |
| 3-Combo | | | | | | | | | | ○ | | | | | | | | | | | | | | |
| Summons | | | | | | | ○ | | | | | | | | | | | | | | | | | |
| Grotto | | | | | | | | | | | | | ○ | | | | | | | | | | | |
| Pit | | | | | | | | | | | | | | | | | | ○ | ○ | | | | | |
| Piercing H | | | ○ | ○ | | | | | | | | | | | | | | ○ | | | | ○ | | |
| Free | ✓ | ✓ | | | | | | | | | ✓ | | | | | | | | | | | | | ✓ |

● major   ○ minor   ✓ taboo free

# Part-3: Personalizing the Facing (仙命宜忌)

## Year Pillar: 戊申 (1908, 1968, 2028, 2088...)   nà yīn element: Earth

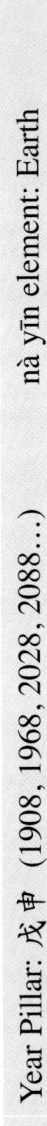

**Sitting Mountain**

|  | 壬 | 子 | 癸 | 丑 | 艮 | 寅 | 甲 | 卯 | 乙 | 辰 | 巽 | 巳 | 丙 | 午 | 丁 | 未 | 坤 | 申 | 庚 | 酉 | 辛 | 戌 | 乾 | 亥 |
|---|---|---|---|---|---|---|---|---|---|---|---|---|---|---|---|---|---|---|---|---|---|---|---|---|
| **Clash** |  |  |  |  |  | ● |  |  |  |  |  |  |  |  |  |  |  |  |  |  |  |  |  |  |
| **Killings** |  |  |  |  |  |  |  |  |  |  |  | ● | ● | ● | ● |  |  |  |  |  |  |  |  |  |
| **Direct K** |  |  |  |  |  |  |  |  |  |  |  |  | ● | ● |  |  |  |  |  |  |  |  |  |  |
| **Punish** |  |  |  |  |  |  |  |  |  |  |  | ● |  |  |  |  |  |  |  |  |  |  |  |  |
| **Seated** |  |  |  |  |  |  |  |  |  |  |  |  |  |  |  |  |  | ● |  |  |  |  |  |  |
| **Harm** |  |  |  |  |  |  |  |  |  |  |  |  |  |  |  |  |  |  |  |  |  |  |  | ● |
| **Retreat** | ○ | ○ | ○ | ○ | ○ |  |  |  |  |  |  |  |  |  |  |  |  |  |  |  |  |  |  |  |
| **3-Combo** | ○ |  |  |  |  |  |  |  |  | ○ |  |  |  |  |  |  |  |  |  |  |  |  |  |  |
| **Summons** |  |  |  |  |  |  |  |  |  |  |  |  |  |  |  |  |  |  |  |  |  | ○ |  |  |
| **Grotto** |  |  |  |  |  |  |  |  |  |  |  |  |  |  |  | ○ |  |  |  |  |  |  |  |  |
| **Pit** |  |  |  |  |  |  |  |  |  |  |  |  |  |  |  |  |  |  | ○ |  |  |  |  |  |
| **Piercing H** |  | ○ | ○ | ○ | ○ |  |  |  |  |  | ○ |  |  |  |  |  |  |  |  |  |  |  |  |  |
| **Free** | ✓ |  |  |  |  |  |  |  |  |  |  |  |  |  |  |  |  |  |  |  | ✓ | ✓ | ✓ | ✓ |

● major   ○ minor   ✓ taboo free

# Part-3: Personalizing the Facing (仙命宜忌)

**Year Pillar: 己酉 (1909, 1969, 2029, 2089…)**     **nà yīn element: Earth**

**Sitting Mountain**

| | 壬 | 子 | 癸 | 丑 | 艮 | 寅 | 甲 | 卯 | 乙 | 辰 | 巽 | 巳 | 丙 | 午 | 丁 | 未 | 坤 | 申 | 庚 | 酉 | 辛 | 戌 | 乾 | 亥 |
|---|---|---|---|---|---|---|---|---|---|---|---|---|---|---|---|---|---|---|---|---|---|---|---|---|
| Clash |  |  |  |  |  |  |  | ● |  |  |  |  |  |  |  |  |  |  |  |  |  |  |  |  |
| Killings |  |  |  |  |  | ● | ● | ● | ● | ● |  |  |  |  |  |  |  |  |  |  |  |  |  |  |
| Direct K |  |  |  |  |  |  |  | ● |  | ● |  |  |  |  |  |  |  |  |  |  |  |  |  |  |
| Punish |  |  |  |  |  |  |  |  |  |  |  |  |  |  |  |  |  |  |  | ● |  |  |  |  |
| Seated |  |  |  |  |  |  |  |  |  |  |  |  |  |  |  |  |  |  |  | ● |  |  |  |  |
| Harm |  |  |  |  |  |  |  |  |  |  |  |  |  |  |  |  |  |  |  |  |  | ● |  |  |
| Retreat | ○ | ○ | ○ |  |  |  |  |  |  |  |  |  |  |  |  |  |  |  |  |  |  |  |  |  |
| 3-Combo |  |  |  | ○ |  |  |  |  |  |  |  | ○ |  |  |  |  |  |  |  |  |  |  |  |  |
| Summons |  |  |  |  |  |  |  |  |  |  |  |  |  |  |  |  |  | ○ |  |  |  |  |  |  |
| Grotto |  |  |  |  |  |  |  |  |  |  |  |  |  |  |  |  |  |  | ○ |  |  |  |  |  |
| Pit |  |  |  |  |  |  |  |  |  |  |  |  |  |  |  |  |  |  |  |  | ○ |  |  |  |
| Piercing H |  |  |  |  | ○ |  | ○ |  | ○ |  | ○ |  |  |  |  |  |  |  |  |  |  |  |  |  |
| Free |  | ✓ |  |  |  |  |  |  |  |  |  |  |  |  |  |  |  |  |  |  |  |  |  |  |

● major   ○ minor   ✓ taboo free

# Part-3: Personalizing the Facing (仙命宜忌)

**Year Pillar: 庚戌 (1910, 1970, 2030, 2090…)**    **nà yīn element: Metal**

### Sitting Mountain

| | 壬 | 子 | 癸 | 丑 | 艮 | 寅 | 甲 | 卯 | 乙 | 辰 | 巽 | 巳 | 丙 | 午 | 丁 | 未 | 坤 | 申 | 庚 | 酉 | 辛 | 戌 | 乾 | 亥 |
|---|---|---|---|---|---|---|---|---|---|---|---|---|---|---|---|---|---|---|---|---|---|---|---|---|
| **Clash** | ● | | | | | | | | | | | | | | | | | | | | | | | |
| **Killings** | | ● | ● | ● | | | | | | | | | | | | | | | | | | | | |
| **Direct K** | | ● | ● | | | | | | | | | | | | | | | | | | | | | |
| **Punish** | | | ● | | | | | | | | | | | | | | | | | | | | | |
| **Seated** | | | | | | | | | | | | | ● | | | | | | | | | ● | | |
| **Harm** | | | | | | | | | | | | | | | | | | | | | ● | | | |
| **Retreat** | | | | | | | | | | | | | | | ○ | ○ | ○ | ○ | ○ | | | | | |
| **3-Combo** | | | | | | | | | | | | | | ○ | | | | | | | | | | |
| **Summons** | | | | | | | | | | | | ○ | | | | | | | | ○ | | | | |
| **Grotto** | | | | | | | | | | | | | | | | | | | | | | | ○ | |
| **Pit** | | | | | | | | | | | | | | ○ | ○ | ○ | | | | | | | | |
| **Piercing H** | | | | | | | | | | | | ○ | | | | ○ | | | | | | | | |
| **Free** | | | | ✓ | ✓ | ✓ | ✓ | | | | | | | | | | | | | | | | | ✓ |

● major   ○ minor   ✓ taboo free

# Part-3: Personalizing the Facing (仙命宜忌)

**Year Pillar: 辛亥 (1911, 1971, 2031, 2091…)**     **nà yīn element: Metal**

### Sitting Mountain

| | 壬 | 子 | 癸 | 丑 | 艮 | 寅 | 甲 | 卯 | 乙 | 辰 | 巽 | 巳 | 丙 | 午 | 丁 | 未 | 坤 | 申 | 庚 | 酉 | 辛 | 戌 | 乾 | 亥 |
|---|---|---|---|---|---|---|---|---|---|---|---|---|---|---|---|---|---|---|---|---|---|---|---|---|
| **Clash** | | | | | | | | | | | | ● | | | | | | | | | | | | |
| **Killings** | | | | | | | | | | | | | | | | | | | | | | | | |
| **Direct K** | | | | | | | | | | | | | | | | | | | | | | | | |
| **Punish** | | | | | | | | | | | | | | | | | | | | | | ● | ● | |
| **Seated** | | | | | | | | | | | | | | | | | | | | ● | ● | ● | | ● |
| **Harm** | | | | | | | | | | | | | | | | | | ● | | | | | | |
| **Retreat** | | | | | | | | | | | | ○ | ○ | ○ | ○ | ○ | | | | | | | | |
| **3-Combo** | | | | | | | | ○ | | | | | | | | ○ | | | | | | | | |
| **Summons** | | | | | | | ○ | | | | | | | | | | | | | | | | | |
| **Grotto** | | | | | | | | | | | | | | | | | | | | ○ | | | | |
| **Pit** | ○ | | | | | | | | | | | | | | | | | | | | | | | |
| **Piercing H** | | | | | | | | | | | | | | | | | | | | ○ | ○ | ○ | ○ | |
| **Free** | ✓ | ✓ | ✓ | ✓ | | | | | | | | | | | | | | | | | | | | ✓ |

● major    ○ minor    ✓ taboo free

# Part-3: Personalizing the Facing (仙命宜忌)

**Year Pillar: 壬子 (1912, 1972, 2032, 2092…)**

**nà yīn element: Wood**

**Sitting Mountain**

| | 壬 | 子 | 癸 | 丑 | 艮 | 寅 | 甲 | 卯 | 乙 | 辰 | 巽 | 巳 | 丙 | 午 | 丁 | 未 | 坤 | 申 | 庚 | 酉 | 辛 | 戌 | 乾 | 亥 |
|---|---|---|---|---|---|---|---|---|---|---|---|---|---|---|---|---|---|---|---|---|---|---|---|---|
| Clash |  |  |  |  |  |  |  |  |  |  |  |  |  |  |  |  |  |  |  |  |  |  |  |  |
| Killings |  |  |  |  |  |  |  |  |  |  |  |  | ● | ● | ● |  |  |  |  |  |  |  |  |  |
| Direct K |  |  |  |  |  |  |  |  |  |  |  |  |  | ● |  |  |  |  |  |  |  |  |  |  |
| Punish |  |  |  |  |  |  |  |  | ● |  |  |  |  |  |  |  |  |  |  |  |  |  |  |  |
| Seated |  | ● |  |  |  |  |  |  |  |  |  |  |  |  |  |  |  |  |  |  |  |  |  |  |
| Harm |  |  |  |  |  |  |  |  |  |  |  |  |  | ● |  |  |  |  |  |  |  |  |  |  |
| Retreat |  |  |  | ○ | ○ | ○ | ○ | ○ | ○ |  |  |  |  |  |  |  |  |  |  |  |  |  |  |  |
| 3-Combo |  |  |  |  |  |  |  |  |  | ○ |  |  |  |  |  |  |  |  |  |  |  |  |  |  |
| Summons |  |  |  |  |  |  |  |  |  |  |  |  |  |  |  |  |  |  |  |  |  | ○ |  |  |
| Grotto | ○ |  |  |  |  |  |  |  |  |  |  |  |  |  |  |  |  |  |  |  |  |  |  |  |
| Pit |  |  | ○ |  |  |  |  |  |  |  |  |  |  |  |  |  |  |  |  |  |  |  |  |  |
| Piercing H |  |  |  |  |  |  |  |  |  |  |  |  |  |  |  |  |  | ○ | ○ | ○ | ○ | ○ | ○ |  |
| Free |  |  |  |  |  |  |  |  |  |  |  | ✓ |  |  |  |  |  | ✓ |  |  |  | ✓ |  |  |

● major    ○ minor    ✓ taboo free

# Part-3: Personalizing the Facing (仙命宜忌)

**Year Pillar:** 癸丑 (1913, 1973, 2033, 2093…)  **nà yīn element:** Wood

### Sitting Mountain

| | 壬 | 子 | 癸 | 丑 | 艮 | 寅 | 甲 | 卯 | 乙 | 辰 | 巽 | 巳 | 丙 | 午 | 丁 | 未 | 坤 | 申 | 庚 | 酉 | 辛 | 戌 | 乾 | 亥 |
|---|---|---|---|---|---|---|---|---|---|---|---|---|---|---|---|---|---|---|---|---|---|---|---|---|
| Clash | | | | | | | | | | | | | | | | ● | | | | | | | | |
| Killings | | | | | | ● | ● | ● | ● | | | | | | | | | | | | | | | |
| Direct K | | | | | | | | ● | | | | | | | | | | | | | | | | |
| Punish | | | | | | | | | | | | | | | | | | | | | | ● | | |
| Seated | | | | ● | | | | | | | | | | | | | | | | | | | | |
| Harm | | | | | | | | | | | | | | ● | | | | | | | | | | |
| Retreat | ○ | ○ | ○ | | | | | | | | | | | | | | | | | | | | | |
| 3-Combo | | | | | | | | | | | | ○ | | | | | | | | | | | | |
| Summons | | | | | | | | | | | | | | | | | | ○ | | | | | | |
| Grotto | | | ○ | | | | | | | | | | | | | | | | | | | | | |
| Pit | | | | | | | | | | | | | | | ○ | | | | | | | | | |
| Piercing H | | | | | | | | | | | | | | | | | | | ○ | ○ | ○ | ○ | ○ | ○ |
| Free | | | | | | | | | | | ✓ | | ✓ | | ✓ | | ✓ | | | | | | | |

● major  ○ minor  ✓ taboo free

# Part-3: Personalizing the Facing (仙命宜忌)

**Year Pillar: 甲寅 (1914, 1974, 2034, 2094…)**

**nà yīn element: Water**

### Sitting Mountain

| | 壬 | 子 | 癸 | 丑 | 艮 | 寅 | 甲 | 卯 | 乙 | 辰 | 巽 | 巳 | 丙 | 午 | 丁 | 未 | 坤 | 申 | 庚 | 酉 | 辛 | 戌 | 乾 | 亥 |
|---|---|---|---|---|---|---|---|---|---|---|---|---|---|---|---|---|---|---|---|---|---|---|---|---|
| Clash | | | | | | | | | | | | | | | | | | ● | | | | | | |
| Killings | | ● | | ● | | | | | | | | | | | | | | | | | | | | ● |
| Direct K | | ● | | | | | | | | | | | | | | | | | | | | | | |
| Punish | | | | | | | | | | | | ● | | | | | | | | | | | | |
| Seated | | | | | | ● | | | | | | | | | | | | | | | | | | |
| Harm | | | | | | | | | | | | ● | | | | | | | | | | | | |
| Retreat | | | | | | | | | | ○ | ○ | ○ | ○ | | ○ | ○ | | | | | | | | |
| 3-Combo | | | | | | | | | | | | | | ○ | | | | | | | | ○ | | |
| Summons | | | | | | | | | | | | ○ | | | | | | | | | | | | |
| Grotto | | | | | | | | ○ | | | | | | | | | | | | | | | | |
| Pit | | | | | | | | | | ○ | | | | | | | | | | | | | | |
| Piercing H | | | | | | | | | | | | | | | | ○ | | | | | | ○ | | |
| Free | ✓ | | | | | | | | | | | | | ✓ | | | ✓ | | | ✓ | | | | ✓ |

● major   ○ minor   ✓ taboo free

# Part-3: Personalizing the Facing (仙命宜忌)

**Year Pillar: 乙卯 (1915, 1975, 2035, 2095…)  nà yīn element: Water**

## Sitting Mountain

| | 壬 | 子 | 癸 | 丑 | 艮 | 寅 | 甲 | 卯 | 乙 | 辰 | 巽 | 巳 | 丙 | 午 | 丁 | 未 | 坤 | 申 | 庚 | 酉 | 辛 | 戌 | 乾 | 亥 |
|---|---|---|---|---|---|---|---|---|---|---|---|---|---|---|---|---|---|---|---|---|---|---|---|---|
| Clash | | | | | | | | | | | | | | | | | | | | • | | | | |
| Killings | | | | | | | | | | | | | | | | | | | | | • | • | | |
| Direct K | | | | | | | | | | | | | | | | | | | | | • | | | |
| Punish | | • | | | | | | | | | | | | | | | | | | | | | | |
| Seated | | | | | | | | • | | | | | | | | | | | | | | | | |
| Harm | | | | | | | | | | • | | | | | | | | | | | | | | |
| Retreat | | | | | | | | | | ○ | ○ | ○ | ○ | ○ | | | | | | | | ○ | | ○ |
| 3-Combo | | | | | | | | | | | | | | | | ○ | | | | | | | | ○ |
| Summons | | | | | | ○ | | | | | | | | | | | | | | | | | | |
| Grotto | | | | | | | | ○ | | | | | | | | | | | | | | | | |
| Pit | | | | | | | | | | | | ○ | | | | | | | | | | | | |
| Piercing H | | | | ○ | ○ | | | | | | | | | | | ○ | | | | | | | | |
| Free | ✓ | ✓ | | | | | | | | | | | | | | | | | | | | | | |

● major   ○ minor   ✓ taboo free

# Part-3: Personalizing the Facing (仙命宜忌)

**Year Pillar: 丙辰 (1916, 1976, 2036, 2096…)    nà yīn element: Earth**

### Sitting Mountain

| | 壬 | 子 | 癸 | 丑 | 艮 | 寅 | 甲 | 卯 | 乙 | 辰 | 巽 | 巳 | 丙 | 午 | 丁 | 未 | 坤 | 申 | 庚 | 酉 | 辛 | 戌 | 乾 | 亥 |
|---|---|---|---|---|---|---|---|---|---|---|---|---|---|---|---|---|---|---|---|---|---|---|---|---|
| **Clash** | | | | | | | | | | | | | | | | | | | | | | ● | | |
| **Killings** | | | | | | | | | | | | ● | ● | ● | ● | ● | | | | | | | | |
| **Direct K** | | | | | | | | | | | | | ● | | | ● | | | | | | | | |
| **Punish** | | | | | | | | | | ● | | ● | | | | | | | | | | | | |
| **Seated** | | | | | | | | | | ● | | | | | | | | | | | | | | |
| **Harm** | | | | | | | | | ● | | | | | | | | | | | | | | | |
| **Retreat** | ○ | ○ | ○ | ○ | ○ | | | | | | | | | | | | | | | | | | | |
| **3-Combo** | | | | | ○ | | | | | | | | | | | | | | | | | | | |
| **Summons** | | | | | | | | | | | | | | | | | | ○ | | | | | | |
| **Grotto** | | | | | | | | | | | ○ | | | | | | | | | | | | | |
| **Pit** | | | | | | | | | | ○ | ○ | ○ | | | | | | | | | | | | |
| **Piercing H** | | | | | | | | | | | ○ | | | | | | | | | | | | | ○ |
| **Free** | ✓ | | | | | | | | | | | | | | | ✓ | | | | ✓ | ✓ | ✓ | ✓ | ✓ |

● major    ○ minor    ✓ taboo free

# Part-3: Personalizing the Facing (仙命宜忌)

**Year Pillar: 丁巳 (1917, 1977, 2037, 2097…)     nà yīn element: Earth**

### Sitting Mountain

| | 壬 | 子 | 癸 | 丑 | 艮 | 寅 | 甲 | 卯 | 乙 | 辰 | 巽 | 巳 | 丙 | 午 | 丁 | 未 | 坤 | 申 | 庚 | 酉 | 辛 | 戌 | 乾 | 亥 |
|---|---|---|---|---|---|---|---|---|---|---|---|---|---|---|---|---|---|---|---|---|---|---|---|---|
| Clash      |   |   |   |   |   |   |   |   |   |   |   |   |   |   |   |   |   |   |   |   |   |   |   | ● |
| Killings   |   |   |   |   |   | ● | ● | ● | ● |   |   |   |   |   |   |   |   |   |   |   |   |   |   |   |
| Direct K   |   |   |   |   |   |   |   |   |   | ● |   |   |   |   |   |   |   |   |   |   |   |   |   |   |
| Punish     |   |   |   |   |   | ● |   |   |   |   |   |   |   |   |   |   |   |   |   |   |   |   |   |   |
| Seated     |   |   |   |   |   |   |   |   |   |   |   | ● |   |   |   |   |   |   |   |   |   |   |   |   |
| Harm       |   |   |   |   |   | ● |   |   |   |   |   |   |   |   |   |   |   |   |   |   |   |   |   |   |
| Retreat    | ○ | ○ | ○ |   |   |   |   |   |   |   |   |   |   |   |   |   |   |   |   |   |   |   |   |   |
| 3-Combo    |   |   |   | ○ |   |   |   |   |   |   |   |   |   |   |   |   |   |   |   |   |   |   |   |   |
| Summons    |   |   |   |   |   |   |   |   |   |   |   |   |   |   |   |   |   |   |   | ○ |   |   |   |   |
| Grotto     |   |   |   |   |   |   |   |   |   |   |   |   |   |   |   |   |   | ○ |   |   |   |   |   |   |
| Pit        |   |   |   |   |   |   |   |   |   |   |   |   |   |   | ○ |   |   |   |   |   |   |   |   |   |
| Piercing H |   |   |   |   |   |   |   |   |   |   |   | ○ |   |   |   |   |   | ○ | ○ | ○ | ○ |   |   |   |
| Free       |   |   |   | ✓ |   |   |   |   |   |   |   |   |   | ✓ | ✓ | ✓ |   |   |   |   | ✓ |   | ✓ |   |

● major     ○ minor     ✓ taboo free

# Part-3: Personalizing the Facing (仙命宜忌)

**Year Pillar: 戊午 (1918, 1978, 2038, 2098…)**  
**nà yīn element: Fire**

### Sitting Mountain

| | 壬 | 子 | 癸 | 丑 | 艮 | 寅 | 甲 | 卯 | 乙 | 辰 | 巽 | 巳 | 丙 | 午 | 丁 | 未 | 坤 | 申 | 庚 | 酉 | 辛 | 戌 | 乾 | 亥 |
|---|---|---|---|---|---|---|---|---|---|---|---|---|---|---|---|---|---|---|---|---|---|---|---|---|
| Clash |  | ● |  |  |  |  |  |  |  |  |  |  |  |  |  |  |  |  |  |  |  |  |  |  |
| Killings |  | ● | ● | ● |  |  |  |  |  |  |  |  |  |  |  |  |  |  |  |  |  |  |  |  |
| Direct K |  |  |  | ● |  |  |  |  |  |  |  |  |  |  |  |  |  |  |  |  |  |  |  |  |
| Punish |  |  |  |  |  |  |  |  |  |  |  |  | ● | ● |  |  |  |  |  |  |  |  |  |  |
| Seated |  |  |  |  |  |  |  |  |  |  |  |  |  |  |  |  |  |  |  |  |  |  |  |  |
| Harm |  |  |  |  |  |  |  |  |  |  |  |  |  |  |  | ● |  |  |  |  |  |  |  |  |
| Retreat |  |  |  |  |  |  |  |  |  |  |  |  |  | ○ | ○ | ○ | ○ |  |  |  |  |  |  |  |
| 3-Combo |  |  |  |  | ○ |  |  |  |  |  |  |  |  |  |  |  |  |  |  |  |  |  |  |  |
| Summons |  |  |  |  |  |  |  |  |  |  | ○ |  |  |  |  |  |  |  |  |  |  |  |  |  |
| Grotto |  |  |  |  |  |  |  |  |  |  |  |  | ○ |  |  |  |  |  |  |  |  |  |  |  |
| Pit |  |  |  |  |  |  |  |  |  |  |  |  |  |  |  | ○ |  |  |  |  |  |  |  |  |
| Piercing H | ○ | ○ | ○ |  |  |  |  |  |  |  |  |  |  |  |  |  |  |  |  |  |  |  |  |  |
| Free |  | ✓ |  |  |  |  |  | ✓ |  | ✓ |  | ✓ |  |  |  |  |  |  |  | ✓ |  | ✓ |  | ✓ |

● major   ○ minor   ✓ taboo free

# Part-3: Personalizing the Facing (仙命宜忌)

**Year Pillar: 乙未 (1919, 1979, 2039, 2099...)**

**nà yīn element: Fire**

## Sitting Mountain

| | 壬 | 子 | 癸 | 丑 | 艮 | 寅 | 甲 | 卯 | 乙 | 辰 | 巽 | 巳 | 丙 | 午 | 丁 | 未 | 坤 | 申 | 庚 | 酉 | 辛 | 戌 | 乾 | 亥 | Free |
|---|---|---|---|---|---|---|---|---|---|---|---|---|---|---|---|---|---|---|---|---|---|---|---|---|---|
| Clash | | | | ● | | | | | | | | | | | | | | | | | | | | | |
| Killings | | | | | | | | | ● | ● | ● | | | | | | | | | | | | | | |
| Direct K | | | | | | | | | ● | | | | | | | | | | | | | | | | |
| Punish | | | | | | ● | | | | | | | | | | | | | | | | | | | |
| Seated | | | | | | | | | | | | | ● | | | | | | | | | | | | |
| Harm | | ● | | | | | | | | | | | | | | | | | | | | | | | |
| Retreat | | | | | | | | | ○ | ○ | ○ | ○ | ○ | ○ | ○ | | | | | | | | | | ✓ |
| 3-Combo | | | | | | | | ○ | | | | | | | | | | | | | | | | | ✓ |
| Summons | | | | | | | | | | | | | ○ | | | | | | | | | | | | ✓ |
| Grotto | | | | | | | | | | | | | | | | | ○ | | | | | | | | |
| Pit | | | | | | | | | | | | | | | | | | | ○ | | | | | | |
| Piercing H | ○ | ○ | ○ | | | | | | | | | | | | | | | | | | | | | | |
| Free | | | | | | | | | | | | | | | | | | | | | | | | | ✓ |

● major    ○ minor    ✓ taboo free

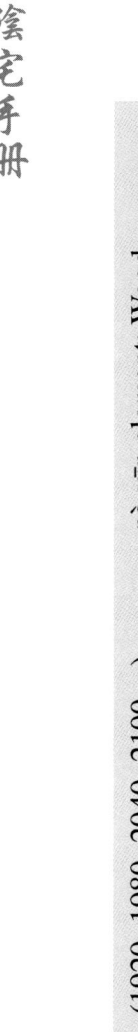

# Part-3: Personalizing the Facing (仙命宜忌)

**Year Pillar: 庚申 (1920, 1980, 2040, 2100…)**   **nà yīn element: Wood**

### Sitting Mountain

| | 壬 | 子 | 癸 | 丑 | 艮 | 寅 | 甲 | 卯 | 乙 | 辰 | 巽 | 巳 | 丙 | 午 | 丁 | 未 | 坤 | 申 | 庚 | 酉 | 辛 | 戌 | 乾 | 亥 |
|---|---|---|---|---|---|---|---|---|---|---|---|---|---|---|---|---|---|---|---|---|---|---|---|---|
| Clash | | | | | | ● | | | | | | | | | | | | | | | | | | |
| Killings | | | | | | | | | | | | ● | ● | ● | ● | | | | | | | | | |
| Direct K | | | | | | | | | | | | | ● | | | | | | | | | | | |
| Punish | | | | | | | | | | | | | ● | | | | | | | | | | | |
| Seated | | | | | | | | | | | | | | | | | | ● | | | | | | |
| Harm | | | | | | | | | | | | | | | | | | | | | | | | ● |
| Retreat | ○ | ○ | ○ | ○ | | | | | | | | | | | | | | | | | | | | |
| 3-Combo | ○ | | | | | | | | | ○ | | | | | | | | | | | | | | |
| Summons | | | | | | | | | | | | | | | | | | | | | ○ | | | |
| Grotto | | | | | | | | | | | | | | | | | ○ | | | | | | | |
| Pit | | | | | | | | | | | | | | | | | | ○ | | ○ | | | | |
| Piercing H | | | | | | | | | | | | | | | | | | ○ | | ○ | ○ | ○ | ○ | ○ |
| Free | ✓ | ✓ | | | | | | | | | | ✓ | | | | | | | | | | ✓ | | |

● major    ○ minor    ✓ taboo free

# Part-3: Personalizing the Facing (仙命宜忌)

**Year Pillar:** 辛酉 (1921, 1981, 2041, 2101…)  nà yīn element: Wood

**Sitting Mountain**

| | 壬 | 子 | 癸 | 丑 | 艮 | 寅 | 甲 | 卯 | 乙 | 辰 | 巽 | 巳 | 丙 | 午 | 丁 | 未 | 坤 | 申 | 庚 | 酉 | 辛 | 戌 | 乾 | 亥 |
|---|---|---|---|---|---|---|---|---|---|---|---|---|---|---|---|---|---|---|---|---|---|---|---|---|
| Clash | | | | | | | | ● | | | | | | | | | | | | | | | | |
| Killings | | | | | ● | ● | ● | ● | | | | | | | | | | | | | | | | |
| Direct K | | | | | | | | | ● | ● | | | | | | | | | | | | | | |
| Punish | | | | | | | | | | | | | | | | | | | | ● | | | | |
| Seated | | | | | | | | | | | | | | | | | | | | | ● | | | |
| Harm | | | | | | | | | | | | | | | | | | | | | | ● | | |
| Retreat | ○ | ○ | ○ | | | | | | | | | | | | | | | | | | | | | |
| 3-Combo | | | | ○ | | | | | | | | | ○ | | | | | | | | | | | |
| Summons | | | | | | | | | | | | | | | | | | | | | | | | |
| Grotto | | | | | | | | | | | | | | | | | | | ○ | | | | | |
| Pit | | | | | | | | | | | | | | | | | | | | ○ | ○ | | | |
| Piercing H | | | ○ | | | | | | | | | | | | | | | | ○ | ○ | ○ | ○ | ○ | ○ |
| Free | | | | | | | | | | | | | ✓ | | | | | | | | | ✓ ✓ ✓ ✓ ✓ | | |

● major  ○ minor  ✓ taboo free

# Part-3: Personalizing the Facing (仙命宜忌)

**Year Pillar: 壬戌 (1922, 1982, 2042, 2102…)    nà yīn element: Water**

### Sitting Mountain

| | 壬 | 子 | 癸 | 丑 | 艮 | 寅 | 甲 | 卯 | 乙 | 辰 | 巽 | 巳 | 丙 | 午 | 丁 | 未 | 坤 | 申 | 庚 | 酉 | 辛 | 戌 | 乾 | 亥 |
|---|---|---|---|---|---|---|---|---|---|---|---|---|---|---|---|---|---|---|---|---|---|---|---|---|
| **Clash** | | | | | | | | | | ● | | | | | | | | | | | | | | |
| **Killings** | ● | ● | ● | | | | | | | | | | | | | | | | | | | | | |
| **Direct K** | | ● | | | | | | | | | | | | | | | | | | | | | | |
| **Punish** | | | | ● | | | | | | | | | | | | | | | | | | | | |
| **Seated** | | | | | | | | | | | | | | | | | | | | | | ● | | |
| **Harm** | | | | | | | | | | | | | | | | | | | | ● | | | | |
| **Retreat** | | | | | | | | | | | | | | | | ○ | ○ | ○ | ○ | ○ | | | | |
| **3-Combo** | | | | | ○ | | | | | | | | | ○ | | | | | | | | | | |
| **Summons** | | | | | | | | | | | | ○ | | | | | | | | | | | | |
| **Grotto** | | | | | | | | | | | | | | | | | | | | ○ | | | | |
| **Pit** | | | | | | | | | | | | | | | | | | | | | | | ○ | |
| **Piercing H** | | ○ | ○ | | | | | | | ○ | | | | | | ○ | | | | ○ | | ○ | | ○ |
| **Free** | | | | | ✓ | ✓ | ✓ | ✓ | ✓ | | ✓ | ✓ | ✓ | | ✓ | | | | | | ✓ | | | |

● major    ○ minor    ✓ taboo free

# Part-3: Personalizing the Facing (仙命宜忌)

**Year Pillar: 癸亥 (1923, 1983, 2043, 2103...)**      **nà yīn element: Water**

### Sitting Mountain

| | 壬 | 子 | 癸 | 丑 | 艮 | 寅 | 甲 | 卯 | 乙 | 辰 | 巽 | 巳 | 丙 | 午 | 丁 | 未 | 坤 | 申 | 庚 | 酉 | 辛 | 戌 | 乾 | 亥 |
|---|---|---|---|---|---|---|---|---|---|---|---|---|---|---|---|---|---|---|---|---|---|---|---|---|
| **Clash** | | | | | | | | | | | | ● | | | | | | | | | | | | |
| **Killings** | | | | | | | | | | | | | | | | | | ● | | ● | | ● | | |
| **Direct K** | | | | | | | | | | | | | | | | | | | | ● | | | | |
| **Punish** | | | | | | | | | | | | | | | | | | | | | | | | ● ● |
| **Seated** | | | | | | | | | | | | | | | | | | | | | | ● | | |
| **Harm** | | | | | | | | | | | | | | | | | | ● | | | | | | |
| **Retreat** | | | | | | | | | | ○ | ○ | ○ | ○ | ○ | ○ | | | | | | | | | |
| **3-Combo** | | | | | | | | ○ | | | | | | | | ○ | | | | | | | | |
| **Summons** | | | | | | | ○ | | | | | | | | | | | | | | | | | |
| **Grotto** | | | | | | | | | | | | | | | | | | | | | | | ○ | |
| **Pit** | ● | | | | | | | | | | | | | | | | | | | | | | | |
| **Piercing H** | | ○ | ○ | | | | | | | | | | | | | ○ | | | | ○ | | ○ | | |
| **Free** | ✓ | ✓ | | | | | | | | | | | | | ✓ | ✓ | | | | | | | | |

● major    ○ minor    ✓ taboo free

# CHAPTER-3.3
## Gold Divisions

Part-3: Personalizing the Facing (仙命宜忌)

## CHAPTER-3.3
### Gold Divisions

It is timely to introduce 2 other rings of the sān hè luó pán called the "120 Dragons Gold Divisions (一百二十龍分金)" plates. As the name suggests, each of these plates has 120 fine divisions on it. One plate is associated with the 24-Mountains Earth Plate, and is usually placed outside the Earth Plate, 1 or 2 layers away. The other is associated with the 24-Mountains Heaven Plate, and is usually placed next to the latter on the outside. See Fig-11.

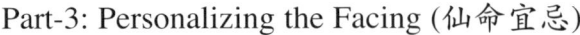

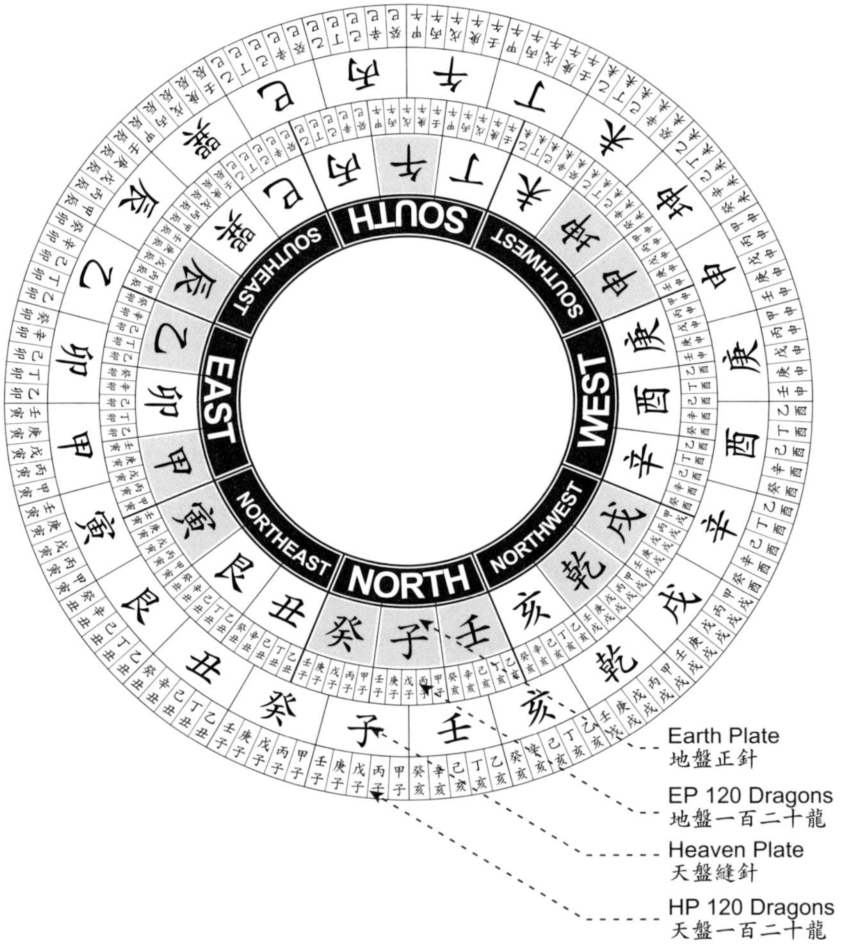

Earth Plate
地盤正針

EP 120 Dragons
地盤一百二十龍

Heaven Plate
天盤縫針

HP 120 Dragons
天盤一百二十龍

**FIG-11: 120 Dragons Gold Divisions**

# Part-3: Personalizing the Facing (仙命宜忌)

As the 2 plates are virtually identical except for an angular shift of 7.5° between them, we shall, for simplicity, discuss the first plate, aptly called the "Earth Plate 120 Dragons" ("EP120D"). Whatever is said of the "EP120D" also applies to its Heaven Plate cousin ("HP120D"). In practice, we would use the "EP120D" first, and only resort to the "HP120D" if we don't get what we want from the "EP120D". More of this later.

To be able to use this plate effectively, one would need at least a professional size luó pán. Nominally called 8.6-chùn (八寸六), the bezel actually measures 26 x 26 cm approx.

Each division on the plate takes up 3° angular spread, and contains a Stem-Branch value, from 甲子 to 癸亥. Each of these values appears twice, separated by 15°. For example, 甲子, 丙子, 戊子, 庚子 and 壬子 appear under 子 Mountain, and are repeated under 癸 Mountain. These make up a total of 120 divisions – hence the name "120 Dragons". The term "Gold Division" is just fancy language that fēngshuǐ masters are so fond of.

Of these 120 divisions, only the ones containing the Stems 丙, 丁, 庚 and 辛 are usable, i.e. no more than 48 usable divisions in total. These are sometimes called "Jewel Lines (珠寶線)". [In this context, the word "line" is synonymous with "division".] Hence in some luó pán, only these 48 divisions are marked, to reduce congestion on the luó pán face.

The important parameter of this plate is in fact the nà yīn elements of the respective Stem-Branch values. Some luó pán are kind enough to mark the elements on an additional ring outside the "EP120D" plate, for convenience. Other luó pán do not consider that necessary as practitioners are expected to know how to derive the nà yīn element of a given Stem-Branch value. See Fig-12 for a simplified "120 Dragons" plate with the nà yīn elements stated.

# Part-3: Personalizing the Facing (仙命宜忌)

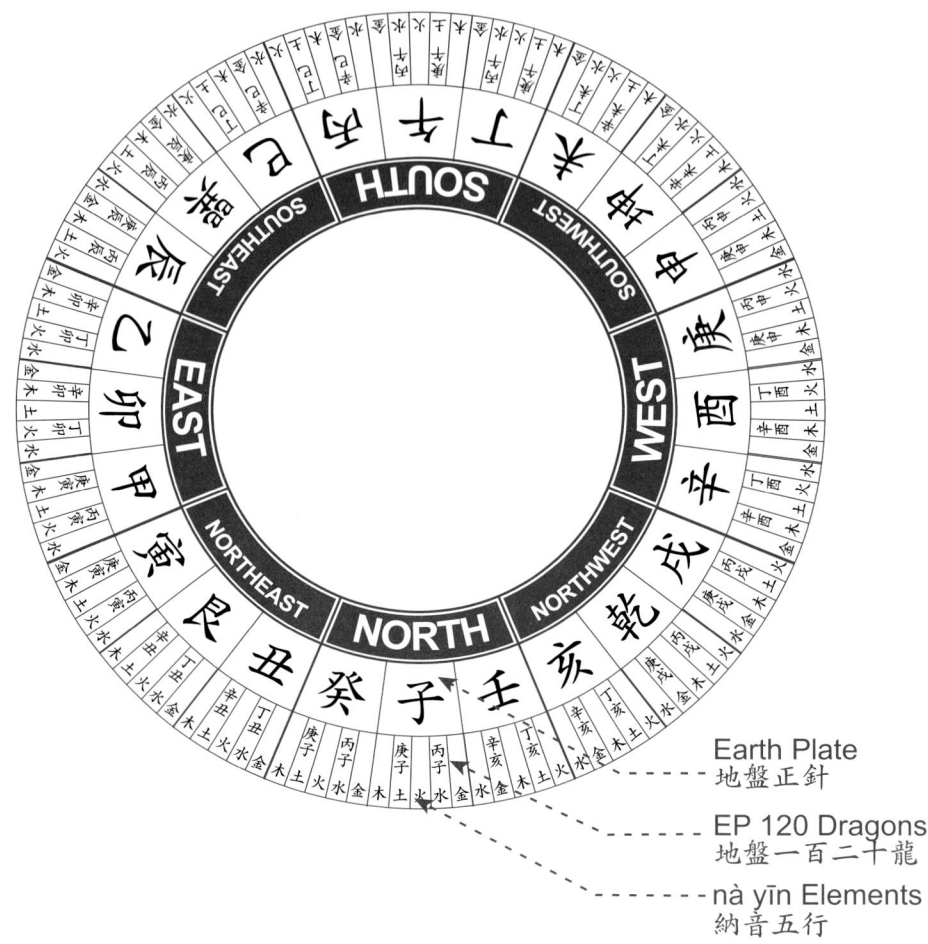

**FIG-12: 120 Dragons Simplified**

But how are these "Gold Divisions" used?

In fact it is just another step in the personalization process.

Suppose we have selected a Sitting Mountain by the rules of Chapter-3.2 above. The "Gold Divisions" formula tells us there are really only 2 tiny (3°) sectors within that Mountain that are usable generally. In addition, we have to check that the nà yīn

# Part-3: Personalizing the Facing (仙命宜忌)

element of the selected "Gold Division" does not counter the nà yīn element of the deceased person's Year Pillar.[13]

The rule is summarized in the following table:

| Year Pillar nà yīn | | "Gold Division" nà yīn |
|---|---|---|
| Wood | should avoid | Metal |
| Fire | should avoid | Water |
| Earth | should avoid | Wood |
| Metal | should avoid | Fire |
| Water | should avoid | Earth |

Take for example a deceased person of Year Pillar 壬子, nà yīn element Wood. By the criteria of Chapter-3.2, a 巽 Sitting Mountain being taboo free would be suitable for him.

Within 巽 Mountain, only the "Gold Divisions" 丙辰 and 庚辰 are usable. 庚辰 is of nà yīn Metal. Metal counters Wood, so 庚辰 is out. That leaves 丙辰 whose nà yīn is Earth. Earth does not counter Wood – hence usable. So if a 巽 Sitting Mountain is indeed selected for a 壬子 person, the tomb should sit on 丙辰 on the "120 Dragons" plate.

---

13 In some texts, this taboo is called "Piercing Tomb (刺穴殺)", which is different from the "Piercing Harm (刺害殺)" listed in Chp-3.2, though the concepts are similar.

We have learnt elsewhere (Chp-2.5) that guest "growing" or "prospering" host is positive, host "countering" guest is also positive, but host "growing" guest and guest "countering" host are negative. Does this concept apply to "Gold Divisions"? The answer is that whilst guest (in this case "Gold Division") "growing" or "prospering" host (Year Pillar) is clearly preferred, it is not achievable at many Mountains. Host "countering" guest is regarded as wealth, hence usable albeit it calls for hard work on the part of the host; and host "growing" guest tends to deplete the host but is at the same time seen as a sentimental relationship, like mother to child. Sometimes the term "mutual growth" is used.

To summarize, if "growing" or "prospering" is unavailable, host "countering" guest is next best; and host "growing" guest is grudgingly accepted. Only guest "countering" host is totally unacceptable.

## Part-3: Personalizing the Facing (仙命宜忌)

Now convention dictates that we refer to a tomb more by its facing than its Sitting, the two being diametrically opposite. An examination of the "120 Dragons" plate reveals that the "Gold Divisions" that are diametrically opposite each other always carry the same nà yīn element. In our example, 丙辰 (Earth) is diametrically opposite 丙戌 (Earth). So instead of saying the tomb sits on 巽 Mountain 丙辰 "Gold Division", it is more common to say the tomb faces 乾 Mountain and 丙戌 "Gold Division" on the "EP120D" plate. The 2 descriptions refer to the same axis.

So where does the "Heaven Plate 120 Dragons" plate come in?

The short answer is that when a satisfactory "Gold Division" is unobtainable with the "EP120D" plate, we turn to the "HP120D" plate to find a remedy.

Take the following example:

As before, deceased person's Year Pillar 壬子, nà yīn element Wood. A 乾 facing (巽 Sitting) Mountain is selected. We know that the only permissible facing on the "EP120D" plate is 丙戌. Now look at the Heaven Plate of the luó pán. It will be seen the tomb axis penetrates the Heaven Plate at 戌. That is fine if the water flow in front of the tomb is from left to right. It would give us a "Weakening" facing of 庚 Metal qì (Chp-2.3 para 6), and that is perfectly acceptable.

But what if the water flow is from right to left? Such a facing would not have met the water requirements of Chapter 2.3

If we were able to use 庚戌, it would have been ok, as the tomb axis would then have penetrated 乾 on the Heaven Plate, and we would have achieved the "Prosperous" facing of 癸 Water qì (Chp-2.3 para 6). Unfortunately we couldn't do that as 庚戌 (Metal) would have been inadmissible for the deceased's 壬子 (Wood) Year Pillar.

## Part-3: Personalizing the Facing (仙命宜忌)

Something needs to be done to resolve the dilemma. The remedy lies in rotating the tomb axis slightly so that it lies smack on the boundary between 庚戌 and 壬戌 on the "EP120D" plate. This is an "Emptiness" line, meaning the qì on this line is neither 庚戌 (Metal) nor 壬戌 (Water).

Now refer to the "HP120D". It will be seen that the tomb axis now lies on the 丙戌 (Earth) "Gold Division" on this plate, which is usable. Now isn't that a simple and elegant solution? See Fig-13.

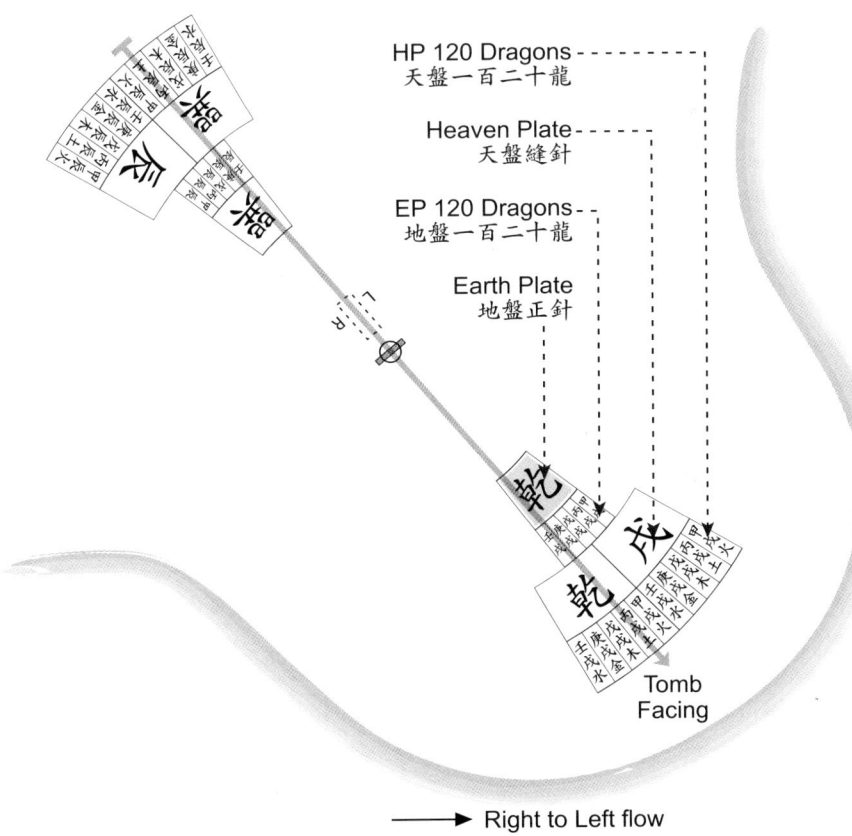

**FIG-13: "EP120D"/"HP120D" usage**

The above case study fully illustrates how the "HP120D" plate is to be used.

# CHAPTER-3.4
## Other Restrictions

Part-3: Personalizing the Facing (仙命宜忌)

## CHAPTER-3.4
## Other Restrictions

Chapters-3.2 & 3.3 discussed the common steps taken to personalize the tomb to the deceased person. These are steps observed by the majority of sān hè practitioners. There are however other restrictions that, in my opinion, are inadequately grounded in theory, and/or are impractical in today's environment. I do not observe these additional restrictions in my practice, but for completeness, I thought I should mention them just in case the reader has come across these terms from other sources.

a. One of them is called "Piercing Blood (刺血殺)". It invokes a rather obscure 5-elements system called "Hóng Fàn 5 Elements (洪范五行)". Under this system the 24-Mountains are assigned elements different from the standard.[14], and a rather complex algorithm is applied, the result of which is that the nà yīn of each Mountain changes with the year.

The nà yīn element of the Sitting Mountain derived in this way is called the "Mountain Luck (山運)", and this is compared with the deceased's Year Pillar nà yīn element. If the "Mountain Luck" element counters the Year Pillar element, the deceased should not be buried into the offending Sitting Mountain that year.

My objections are two-fold: firstly the "Hóng Fàn 5 Elements" is a rather off-beat system; and secondly what does one do if the person dies in a year when his pre-selected burial plot goes through the wrong "Mountain Luck"?

---

14 The "Hóng Fàn 5 Elements" for the 24-Mountains are: 甲寅辰巽戌子辛申 = Water, storage @辰; 艮卯巳 = Wood, storage @未; 午壬丙乙 = Fire, storage @戌; 乾亥酉丁 = Metal, storage @丑; 丑癸坤庚未 = Earth, storage @辰.

# Part-3: Personalizing the Facing (仙命宜忌)

In the old days, it was fairly common to put the sealed casket into temporary storage for months or even years to wait for a desired burial date. This is simply not done today.

b. Another is called "Year Harm (歲害殺)" [different from "Harm (命害)" defined in Chp-3.1 para f]. Here again, for a given Sitting Mountain, an algorithm is applied to the deceased's Year Pillar, and the same is applied to the current year's Stem-Branch value. The nà yīn elements thus obtained are compared, and again the Sitting Mountain's element must not counter the Year Pillar's element.

I am skeptical that the algorithm employed is valid.

c. Yet another restriction is called "4 Sky Chiefs (天罡四殺)". Based on the deceased's Year Branch, certain Sitting Mountains are off limits.[15] if the Branch value of the burial year, month, date or hour happens to correspond with the deceased's "Direct Killing" [Chp-3.1 para c].

There is very little logical or classical support for this claim.

From the practical standpoint, it is hard enough to select a Sitting Mountain, and hence facing, that complies with the earlier chapters and also satisfies the "Dragon" and water requirements of Part-2. We can certainly do without the hassle of these additional restrictions that are highly questionable in themselves.

---

15 The off limits Mountains come in a set of 4: either 甲卯庚辛 or 壬癸丙丁 – hence the name.

# CHAPTER-3.5
## Multiple Occupancy Tombs

Part-3: Personalizing the Facing (仙命宜忌)

## CHAPTER-3.5
### Multiple Occupancy Tombs

Nowadays it is common to have a married couple wanting to be buried together in the same tomb when they die. This is an understandable wish although it is generally not possible to optimize a tomb for 2 different persons. There are of course exceptions, but such happy coincidences are fortuitous rather than planned.

Traditional Chinese society is paternal in character. The male is dominant in death as in life. Unless otherwise instructed by the client, the fēngshuǐ master would therefore personalize the tomb for the husband, and the wife will defer to her husband's best interests. Maybe that's not fair in the eyes of modern society, but as fēngshuǐ practitioners, we do not make the rules but merely implement our client's wishes.

A word of advice: the so-called standard double plot offered in many modern memorial parks is barely large enough to accommodate 2 caskets laid side-by-side. It is almost impossible to tilt the caskets to any appreciable degree in these plots. So if tilting is required, please consider purchasing 2 adjoining double plots, although that would mean doubling the expenses.

Some clients favour large burial plots designed to accommodate the parents and all the siblings in a family. Many modern memorial parks offer and actively promote such family plots for obvious reasons. From the fēngshuǐ perspective, this is not the best solution. Seldom will all the siblings share the same favourable facing as their parents. Compromise is unavoidable in practice.

## Part-3: Personalizing the Facing (仙命宜忌)

In the old days, many wealthy families had their own private burial grounds, but that was a far cry from today's so-called family plots. The old private grounds spread out over a vast area, and within this area, suitable facings could generally be found for each member of the family. Not so with the modern family plot where the freedom to orientate the individual tombs is severely restricted. Again, as fēngshuǐ practitioners we do not make judgments, but merely provide advice if our advice is sought.

# CHAPTER-3.6
## Pre-selecting a Burial Plot

Part-3: Personalizing the Facing (仙命宜忌)

## CHAPTER-3.6
### Pre-selecting a Burial Plot

In ancient China, when a new emperor ascended the throne, one of his first tasks was to look for a burial site for his future use. Upon finding such a site, he would start building the tomb straightaway. Yet for some reason or other, many people today feel uncomfortable even talking about their future resting place, let alone plan for it.

What happens is that when they eventually pass on, the family is thrown into grief and dishevel. A burial plot has to be found quickly. Many families fall victim to unscrupulous salesmen and end up with costly but unsuitable plots.

Fortunately, increasingly more people today have woken up to the reality that pre-selecting one's own burial plot will not hasten one's departure in any way, and is in fact a responsible thing to do. Like estate planning, a pre-selected plot and specific instructions will go a long way to alleviating the uncertainties a bereaved family has to face come that fateful day.

It is now fairly common for financially stable people to purchase their own burial plots well in advance. Some look at it as an investment, for the price of burial land, like any other land, can only appreciate with time. To a large extent the publicity efforts of modern memorial parks have to be thanked for this positive change in outlook.

The criteria for selecting one's own future burial plot are no different from those discussed elsewhere in this book.

# Part-3: Personalizing the Facing (仙命宜忌)

Some people even pre-construct their future tombs like the old emperors, but with today's efficient construction methods, that is perhaps unnecessary, but certainly no harm doing so. It is quite acceptable to leave the plot vacant. Modern memorial park management will take adequate care of the plot, vacant or built-up.

Building a tomb for future use is not to be confused with a certain practice called "Pre-burial (生基)" that has been popular in Taiwan for some time, and is slowly spreading to other lands. A "Pre-burial" involves placing into a small container a living person's clothing article, hair or nail clippings, and the person's bā zì written on a piece of paper, and then burying that container into the tomb on a selected date.

Normally this is done for a person who is critically ill, or is down and out financially. It is claimed that doing so will turn around the person's fortunes, and will even extend his life for 10 years or more. The idea is that the affected person is deemed to have died, buried and reborn.

Is there classical fēngshuǐ support for such a practice? Well, in some old texts, the term "vacant tomb (穴空)" was mentioned. It was stated that certain Incoming Dragons and facings were only suitable for "vacant tombs". This term could have been used to describe "Pre-burial" tombs, but we are not sure.

Personally I do not subscribe to the idea of "Pre-burial", but would recommend without hesitation the advance purchase of one's future resting place.

# Part-4

Ancillary Features

# CHAPTER-4.1
## Water Drainage

Part-4: Ancillary Features

## CHAPTER-4.1
### Water Drainage

Traditional tomb structures have a flat area, usually half-moon shaped, in front of the tombstone where the descendants gather to pay respects to their buried ancestors. This area is usually bounded by a low kerb at the front edge, designed to retain the qì that flows down from the back of the tomb. For practical reasons, the tomb enclosure has to be effectively drained, and from the fēngshuǐ standpoint, the qì needs to be gathered but must never be stagnant.

A hole or a small gap in the front kerb is provided for drainage. The precise location of this drain outlet is regulated by fēngshuǐ guidelines, as follows:

As we have used the "Later Heaven Water Method" to align the tomb, the same method is applied to locate the drain outlet. To recap: we said that the tomb can face either "Prosperous" or "Weakening" [Chp-2.3 para 6]. The rule is that the water within the tomb enclosure should exit at "Weakening" if the tomb faces "Prosperous"; and should exit at "Sick" if the tomb faces "Weakening". The idea is that the spent water should exit as soon as practicable after it has flowed past the tomb facing. Of course if there is a physical obstruction at the preferred location, it is permissible to exit further down the cycle, i.e. at "Death" or "Grave".

In addition, the outlet should be located at a Stem Mountain and not a Branch Mountain. Stem exits are unaffected by annual afflictions such as the "Grand Duke (太歲)" and "3-Killings (三煞)" (at least the 3 major components thereof), and are deemed to be safer.

# Part-4: Ancillary Features

The preferred locations for the drain outlet are tabulated below:

|  | Tomb facing | | Drain outlet | |
|---|---|---|---|---|
| For left-to-right water: | "Prosperous" | 甲, 卯 | "Weakening" | 乙 |
| | | 丙, 午 | | 丁 |
| | | 庚, 酉 | | 辛 |
| | | 壬, 子 | | 癸 |
| | "Weakening" | 辰 | "Sick" | 巽 |
| | | 未 | | 坤 |
| | | 戌 | | 乾 |
| | | 丑 | | 艮 |
| For right-to-left water | "Prosperous" | 艮, 寅 | "Weakening" | 癸* |
| | | 巽, 巳 | | 乙* |
| | | 坤, 申 | | 丁* |
| | | 乾, 亥 | | 辛* |
| | "Weakening" | 癸 | "Sick" | 壬 |
| | | 乙 | | 甲 |
| | | 丁 | | 丙 |
| | | 辛 | | 庚 |

[*There is potential conflict with the "8 Roads" formula in 艮, 巽, 坤 and 乾 facings. See later paragraphs.]

## Part-4: Ancillary Features

In the above table, the "Tomb facing" is based on the Earth Plate, as expected. One may be tempted to think that the "Drain outlet" should be based on the Heaven Plate, as is normal with water measurements, but in this case the "Drain outlets" are also based on the Earth Plate. The reason is that annual afflictions like "Grand Duke" and "3-Killings" are determined by the Earth Plate. So in order to avoid these annual afflictions, it is also necessary to locate the drain outlet according to this plate. All measurements are taken from the centre of the tombstone.

The more fastidious practitioner may wish to locate the exit more precisely such that it sits on a Stem Mountain on the Earth Plate, and at the same time sits on the required Paired-mountains on the Heaven Plate. This is possible but it will mean only one half of the Earth Plate Stem Mountain is usable.

There is one other restriction to observe: the drain outlet must not violate the "8 Roads of Destruction (八路黃泉)" formula. We have seen this formula in Chp-2.3 para 9, but for easy reference the formula is repeated below:

> 庚 or 丁 facing, water must not exit at 坤
> Conversely, 坤 facing, water must not exit at 庚 or 丁
> 乙 or 丙 facing, water must not exit at 巽
> Conversely, 巽 facing, water must not exit at 乙 or 丙
> 甲 or 癸 facing, water must not exit at 艮
> Conversely, 艮 facing, water must not exit at 甲 or 癸
> 辛 or 壬 facing, water must not exit at 乾
> Conversely, 乾 facing, water must not exit at 辛 or 壬

# Part-4: Ancillary Features

Only the Stem facings are affected by this formula. If the "8 Roads" formula is violated, the wealth prospects of the tomb, and hence the descendants, will go down the drain, so to speak.

Take for example a tomb facing 乾, and the water flow is right-to-left. The tomb faces "Prosperous", which means the drain outlet could be at 辛 "Weakening" (see earlier paragraph), but that would violate the "8 Roads" formula. In this case, the drain outlet should be shifted to 庚 "Sick". In a narrow plot, this could present a problem. The practitioner's resourcefulness is called upon to solve the problem.

It should be mentioned that in modern high density cemeteries, and in some cases even elaborate tombs of modern design, there is no kerb to retain the qì at the front. In such cases, there is evidently no qì accumulation and therefore no drain outlet to speak of. Will this impact the tomb fēngshuǐ negatively? I'm afraid there is insufficient evidence to conclude one way or the other.

# CHAPTER-4.2
## Earth Deity

Part-4: Ancillary Features

## CHAPTER-4.2
### Earth Deity

In the majority of traditional Chinese tombs, there is a small shrine for the Earth Deity usually located at one side of the tomb. Strictly speaking, the Earth Deity is a cultural and not a fēngshuǐ feature, but as practitioners we are often asked to locate this shrine properly. This we need to do for good customer relations even if the task is not strictly a fēngshuǐ service.

The Earth Deity is a Daoist feature. According to Daoist beliefs, the Earth Deity represents the guardian of the land in the spirit world. Its presence will deter other unauthorized spirits from occupying or desecrating the plot; in much the same way as a legal resident at a property in our physical world will turn away squatters and other unwelcome visitors.

If the deity is placed at the front half of the tomb, it is called "Earth Queen (后土)". If it is located at the back half of the tomb, it is called "Dragon God (龍神)". That is the correct nomenclature, but such correctitude is largely ignored in common usage, and the Earth Deity is simply called "Earth Queen" irrespective of its location. In fact, "Earth Queen" was originally female. She was supposed to be the spouse of the "Jade Emperor (玉帝)", but today we often see a bearded figure depicted in the shrines!
[Didn't know that females in the Daoist pantheon sported facial hair!]

If an Earth Deity is to be installed, it stands to reason that it should be located at a place of honour. The traditional approach is to apply an ancient poem by the name of "Imperial Carriage Classic for the Door (門樓玉輦經)", variously attributed to Grandmaster Yáng Yún Sōng (楊筠松) or his disciples.

# Part-4: Ancillary Features

A new set of 24 "Gods & Killings" is introduced, and each of the 24-Mountains on the Earth Plate is assigned one of these 24 entities, but the "God" or "Killing" for each Mountain varies depending on the Trigram of the tomb's Sitting Mountain.[16]. 12 of the 24 are positive, the other 12 negative. Clearly the Earth Deity should be located at one of the positive "Gods".

The sequence of the 24 "Gods & Killings" remains fixed, as follows:

"Good Karma (福德)"; "Epidemic (瘟疫)"; "Income (進財)"; "Lingering Illness (長病)"; "Litigation (訴訟)"; "Public Office (官爵)"; "High Status (官貴)"; "Hanged (自吊)"; "Property Luck (旺莊)"; "Good Fortune (興福)"; "Execution Yard (法場)"; "Insanity (顛狂)"; "Slander (口舌)"; "Silk (旺蠶)"; "Property Acquisition (進田)"; "Grief (哭泣)"; "Widow/Orphan (孤寡)"; "Splendor (榮昌); "Premature Death (少亡)"; "Immorality (娼淫)"; "Marriage (姻親)"; "Happiness (歡樂)"; "Utter Defeat (敗絕)"; "Wealth Luck (旺財)".

The names adequately identify the good from the bad.

The location of the first item, "Good Karma", changes with the Sitting Trigram. The sequence then progresses clockwise on the luó pán. The possible locations of the Earth Deity are best described graphically. See Fig-14a ~ h where the allowable Mountains are marked with a ✓.

---

16 戌乾亥 Mountains belong to Trigram 乾; 壬子癸 Trigram 坎; 丑艮寅 Trigram 艮; 甲卯乙 Trigram 震; 辰巽巳 Trigram 巽; 丙午丁 Trigram 離; 未坤申 Trigram 坤; 庚酉辛 Trigram 兌.

Part-4: Ancillary Features

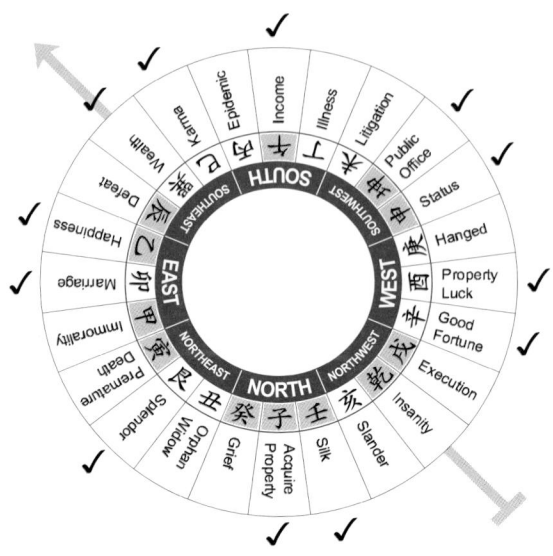

(a) Tomb Sitting: 乾 Qian

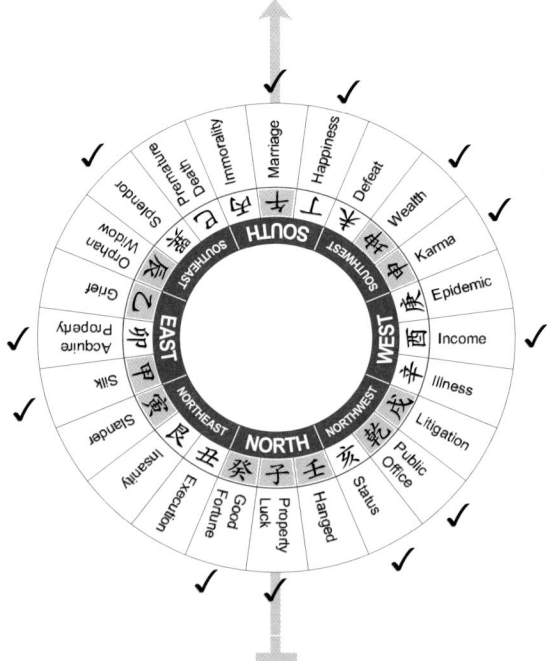

(b) Tomb Sitting: 坎 Kan

**FIG-14a-b: Earth Deity locations**

Part-4: Ancillary Features

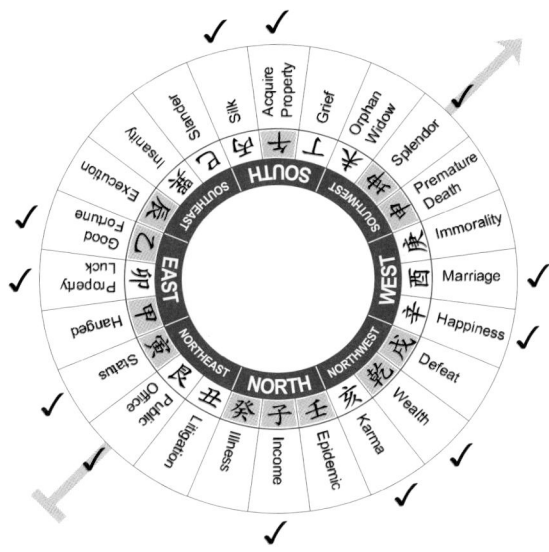

(c) Tomb Sitting: 艮 gen

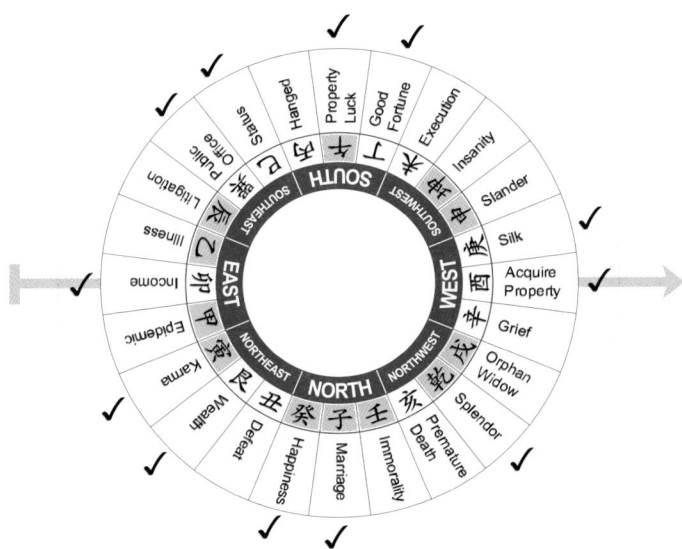

(d) Tomb Sitting: 震 Zhen

**FIG-14c-d: Earth Deity locations**

# Part-4: Ancillary Features

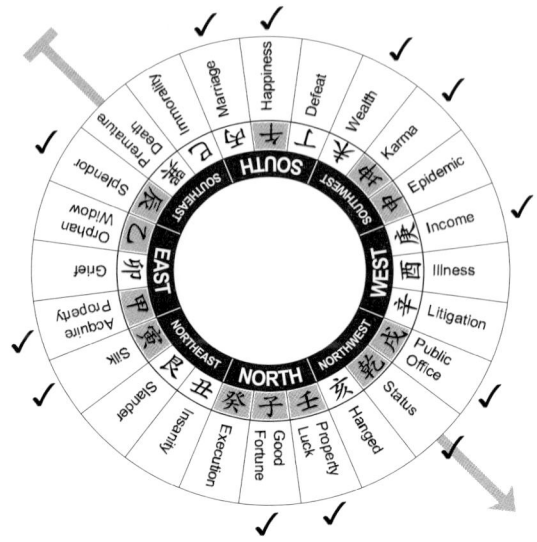

(e) Tomb Sitting: 巽 Xun

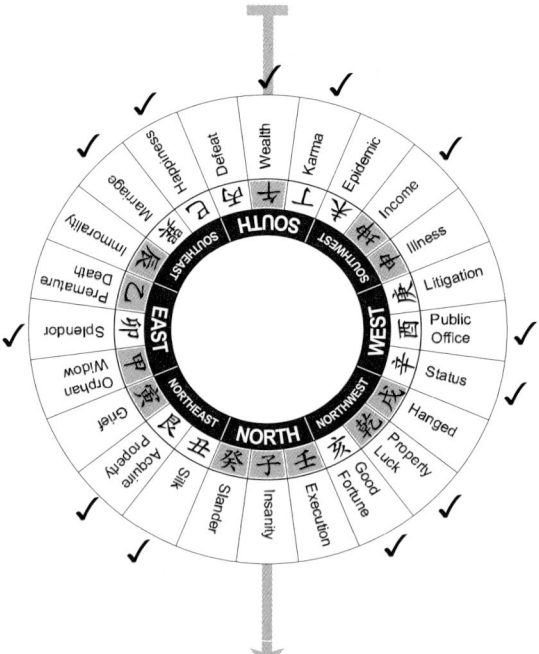

(f) Tomb Sitting: 離 Li

**FIG-14e-f: Earth Deity locations**

Part-4: Ancillary Features

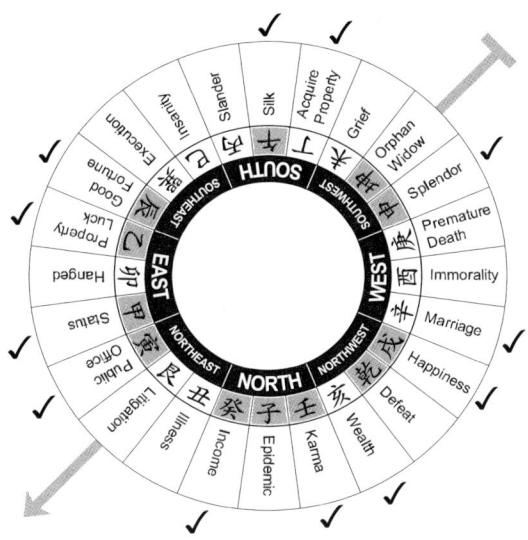

(g) Tomb Sitting: 坤 Kun

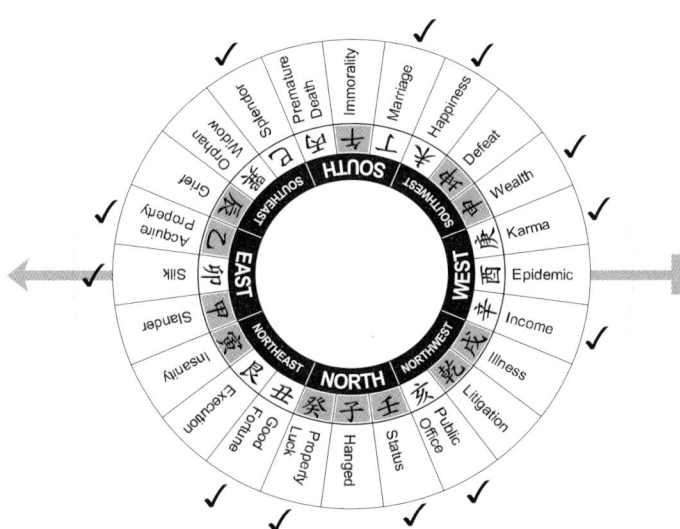

(h) Tomb Sitting: 兑 Dui

**FIG-14g-h: Earth Deity locations**

## Part-4: Ancillary Features

Technically, the reference point should be the centre of the burial plot, but in practice it is more convenient to measure from the tombstone. The Earth Plate is used.

I subscribe to the practice of placing the Earth Deity on the same side of the tomb as the drain outlet [Chp-4.1], but some practitioners may have a different idea.

There is no hard and fast rule governing the facing of the Earth Deity. Normally it is placed to face the same direction as the tombstone, or at right angles to it.

Many modern tombs decided to omit the Earth Deity altogether. This is a decision the family has to make. From the fēngshuǐ perspective, it is not an issue. As mentioned at the beginning of this chapter, the Earth Deity is a cultural more than a fēngshuǐ feature.

# CHAPTER-4.3
## Miscellaneous

Part-4: Ancillary Features

## CHAPTER-4.3
### Miscellaneous

### 1. Offerings Table

In many tomb designs, a raised pedestal is constructed just in front of the tombstone. It may look like a base for the tombstone, but structurally that is not the case. In modern tombs, the tombstone is usually seated on a reinforced concrete plinth hidden from view. The raised pedestal is meant for placing the flowers, food and other offerings that visitors bring to the tomb.

Normally this offerings table is not a fēngshuǐ feature. I only mention it because certain fēngshuǐ schools make use of this table in rather novel ways to achieve their desired fēngshuǐ objectives.

One school I know of tilts the front edge of this table to line up with a desired division on the "72-Dragons" plate of the sān hè luó pán. Used in conjunction with the tomb's side walls (acting as Embraces) and drain outlet, this manoeuvre seeks to control the angles at which the external qì enters and leaves the tomb. This school guards its secrets jealously, and strictly regulates the dissemination of its proprietary knowledge.

Another school tilts the table to compensate for unfriendly Embraces visible from the tomb [Chp-2.5]. The idea is to turn the table to face an "Emptiness Line" between 2 Mountains, so that an unfriendly Embrace will not be able to affect the tomb.

Part-4: Ancillary Features

These manoeuvres are proprietary to certain schools, and are out of mainstream sān hè fēngshuǐ. Not knowing enough, we do not question their effectiveness, but should keep an open mind. At the very least, we should not be confounded by the tilted tables at some of the tombs we visit.

## 2. Neck

In certain tombs, a small and short tunnel like structure, usually of brick, is constructed behind the tombstone below ground level. It is sometimes called a "Dragon Neck (龍頸)", connecting the tombstone to the interior of the tomb. The tombstone is regarded as the tomb's antenna, and the neck serves as a conduit for qì or signals to pass between this antenna and the body of the tomb.

Some practitioners place much emphasis on this neck, but there is scant support for it in classical writings or ancient tombs that have been excavated.

Without further substantiation, we must regard this feature as a peculiar preference of certain practitioners only.

Part-4: Ancillary Features

### 3. Colours

Certain fēngshuǐ practitioners contend that the colour of the tomb structure, and especially the tombstone, is important and have come up with colour schemes to suit tomb orientations or other criteria. However, there is no classical support for this view.

### 4. Dimensions

Some practitioners are adamant that the overall dimensions of the tomb should be guided by auspicious measurements obtained using a "Lǔ Bān Ruler (魯班尺)", sometimes simply called a fēngshuǐ ruler. These same practitioners would insist that yáng house doors, stoves and beds must be tailor made to specific dimensions using this ruler.

The use of the "Lǔ Bān Ruler" has long been discarded by the majority of fēngshuǐ masters today, but there are those who are evidently more nostalgic.

### 5. Boy and Girl

Sometimes one sees a pair of stone or pottery figures, one of a young boy, the other a girl, standing by the tomb as if in attendance. These are not fēngshuǐ features but cultural symbols. The idea is not unlike the page boys and girls at a wedding, a symbol of fertility and the ability to procreate.
[Looks like sex is never far from the Chinese mind, even in death!]

Part-4: Ancillary Features

## 6. Pineapple

In some tombs, at least in Southeast Asia, we see a pineapple plant growing out of the burial mound on top of the tomb. The lower part of a pineapple fruit is planted into the mound when the family visits the tomb, and if this plant takes root and grows, it is taken to be a sign of abundance for the family.

Clearly this is a cultural practice that has nothing to do with fēngshuǐ. In fact it arises from a play on the phonetics of the Fujiàn (Hokkien) dialect. I mentioned it out of curiosity more than anything else.

# CHAPTER-4.4
## Tomb Construction

Part-4: Ancillary Features

## CHAPTER-4.4
### Tomb Construction

Other than the tomb facing and related features discussed in this and earlier chapters, the design and construction of the tomb really has little fēngshuǐ significance.

I do not intend to cover tomb design and construction in any detail in this handbook. Modern tomb designs are simply too varied. Some are severely limited by space, as with the very small plots offered by public cemeteries in densely populated countries. Others cater to the elaborate and ostentatious tastes of the super rich. Yet others prefer a modern design with clean lines. The design does not really matter, as long as the tomb observes certain guidelines, as follows:

a. Drainage must be efficient. The plot must not be waterlogged.

b. If the tomb is located on a hill slope with higher ground at the back, a strong retaining wall is needed at the rear to prevent a collapse of the slope.

c. In very large plots, drains may be incorporated into the tomb design to divert rain water to the sides and then collect at the front, so that the burial mound will not be inundated in a heavy downpour.

d. Side walls are useful for demarcating the plot and helping to gather the qì, albeit these walls do make the tomb look staid. Many modern tombs have decided to omit these walls for space or aesthetic reasons. That is permissible if there are natural landforms serving the function of left and right Embraces.

e. Have a flat area in front of the tombstone for visitors to stand, and also for qì to gather. In a traditional tomb this space is usually half-moon shaped, but there is really no reason why this has to be so.

f. If trees are planted near a tomb, please avoid tree species having large canopies as these trees will also have roots that spread far and wide. There is a danger of such roots dislocating and wrapping round the casket.

g. Whilst it is fashionable to have tomb structures finished in expensive granite slabs or ceramic tiles, these are purely decorative and do not affect the tomb's fēngshuǐ in any way. Neither do human or animal sculptures nor decorative frescos have any fēngshuǐ significance.

h. The tomb structure should be examined yearly. Watch out for cracks, potholes and other signs of possible subterranean earth movement. Any defect should be repaired immediately. Any damage to the tombstone, even unusual discoloration on its surface, could be an indication of impending trouble for the family.

Chinese culture sets aside a week in early April for families to visit their ancestors' tombs. This period coincides with the astronomical event "Qīng Míng (清明)" (meaning bright and clear) that denotes the beginning of the 3$^{rd}$ solar month in the Chinese calendar. For many people, the visit has become a yearly ritual and a social event that brings together the extended family, which is of course a good thing. But from the fēngshuǐ viewpoint, there is really no need to squeeze the visit into this one week. Any day is a good day to visit one's ancestors' tombs, pay one's respects, and inspect the tomb maintenance.

Part-4: Ancillary Features

Fig-15 shows a traditional style of tomb popular with yesteryear's rich and famous in Southern China, Taiwan and parts of Southeast Asia. It is interesting to see how the designer created artificial features in the microcosm of the tomb to mimic natural landforms in the greater exterior.

FIG-15: Traditional Tomb

"Cicada Wings", "Prawn Whiskers", "Goldfish", etc. are fanciful names of landforms that help to drain the land and gather the qì. In this example, such natural landforms are absent, so the tomb designer created his own. To what extent these artificial versions will help is a moot point, but they do make an interesting case-in-point for landform studies.

[In this case, the "Cicada Wings" look more like a bat's wings. Could this be Batman's tomb?]

Of course the design is grossly outmoded for modern taste. I for one would not think of recommending it to my clients! But if one were to examine modern tomb designs, one shouldn't be surprised to find traces of the same idea expressed perhaps in a more subtle way.

### Application Notes

I recommend leaving the tomb design to the experts. Modern memorial parks operate a dedicated department to design, build and maintain the tombs. Leave it to them to discuss the design with the family. At burial grounds managed by non-profit organizations, the service is usually provided by the undertakers. As fēngshui practitioners, our job is just to provide the fēngshui input.

In my practice, I always provide a simple drawing to specify clearly in writing the recommended tombstone facing; casket alignment if different; drain outlet; and Earth Deity location if required. An example is shown in Fig-16. Any competent undertaker should be able to dig a pit to comply with this specification, but I have come across undertakers who fail to follow instructions, inadvertently or otherwise. In any ensuing argument, the drawing will come in very useful.

If I am engaged to perform a full yīn house service, I make it a point to check the burial pit alignment before they put in the brick or prefabricated lining. It will mean an additional trip to the site, but experience has taught me that the extra work is necessary. It will be simply too late to discover that the pit has been dug wrongly only when the funeral party is assembled for the burial ceremony!

## Part-4: Ancillary Features

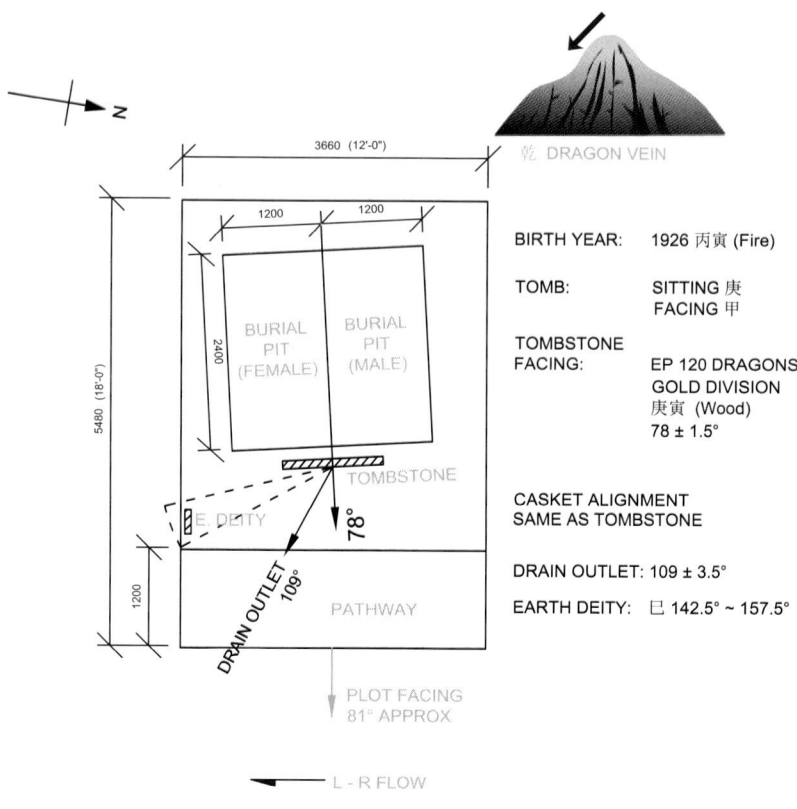

**FIG-16: Typical Specification Drawing**

# Part-5

## Date Selection

# CHAPTER-5.1
## Why Select a Date

Part-5: Date Selection

## CHAPTER-5.1
### Why Select a Date

A burial is no different from people moving into a new house. Just as many people will want to select a good date and time to move into their new home, so too should a burial take place at a favourable date and time. It's all about setting off on a good start.

There is a classical saying that "The veins in the earth may be the source of good fortune, but it is timing that makes it happen (發福由其地脈, 催福出於良辰)".

As this is not a treatise on date selection, the rationale behind the need to select a good date and time will not be belaboured, suffice to say that for any activity to produce its desired result, the trinity of Heaven Earth and Man must be complete. In this case, Heaven is represented by the timing of the burial, Earth by the fēngshuǐ of the tomb, and Man by the characteristics of the deceased.

There are many ways to select a date, and even to learn a single method comprehensively will require a study program much more in depth than this handbook is able to cover. In our present discussions, I assume the reader will have had some exposure to the "Gods & Killings (神煞)" method of date selection, and in particular, the "12 Day Officers (建除十二值神)".

The "Book of Unifying Times & Discerning Dimensions (協紀辨方書)" first published in 1740 under the auspices of Emperor Qián Lóng is generally accepted as the definitive treatise of the "Gods & Killings". Unfortunately this book is hard to read even for seasoned practitioners, but many modern books and study

# Part-5: Date Selection

programs have come to the rescue. The book "Personal Date Selection" by Master Joey Yap is an excellent entry level book that introduces the "12 Day Officers" very well.

The "12 Day Officers" are stated in all "tōng shū (通書)" and Chinese calendars. Simply look up one of these for the Day Officer presiding over any one day.[17]

In the following list of Day Officers, those that are generally suitable for burial are marked with a tick (✓); those that should be avoided with a cross (✗); and the in-betweens with a circle (O):

| | | |
|---|---|---|
| Establish | (建) | ✗ |
| Remove | (除) | O |
| Full | (滿) | ✗ |
| Balance | (平) | O |
| Stable | (定) | O |
| Execute | (執) | ✓ |
| Break | (破) | ✗ |
| Danger | (危) | O |
| Success | (成) | ✓ |
| Receive | (收) | O |
| Open | (開) | O |
| Close | (閉) | ✗ |

---

17 JY Books Sdn Bhd publishes an excellent "tōng shū", in English, each year. Called the "Pro Tong Shu", it is designed for professional use.

## Part-5: Date Selection

If one follows the list strictly, there are very few suitable days[18]. In practice, I would not hesitate to use the days marked ⭕ if certain beneficial "Gods" are present. These include:

"Yearly Virtue (歲德)",
   also called "Duke Virtue"

"Yearly Virtue Combo (歲德合)",
   also called "Duke Virtue Combo"

"Heavenly Virtue (天德)"

"Heavenly Virtue Combo (天德合)"

"Monthly Virtue (月德)"

"Monthly Virtue Combo (月德合)"

"Will of Heaven (天愿)"

"Heavenly Pardon (天赦)"

2 "Killings" to be avoided for burials are:
   "Voluminous Day (重日)"
   "Double Funeral (重喪)"

It is beyond the scope of this handbook to define each of these "Gods & Killings". Please look up the date selection texts. The "Gods & Killings" present on each day are listed in most "tōng shū".

---

18 The grading has been substantially relaxed. The traditional list was much stricter, to the extent of being impractical for modern times.

## Part-5: Date Selection

There are, however, several **important** provisos:

– If the current Day Branch clashes with the birth Year Branch of the deceased, that day is unusable;

– If the current Day Branch clashes with the birth Year Branch of the principal bereaved person, that day should be avoided. Traditionally that would be the eldest son, but nowadays it may be another family member, usually the one who pays the bill;

– If the current date is one day prior to the following astronomical events, that day is unusable:

"Vernal Equinox (春分)"

"Summer Solstice (夏至)"

"Autumnal Equinox (秋分)"

"Winter Solstice (冬至)"

"Coming of Spring (立春)"

"Coming of Summer (立夏)"

"Coming of Autumn (立秋)"

"Coming of Winter (立冬)"

These astronomical events are stated in all "tōng shū" and Chinese calendars.

– If the current date is a "Year Breaker (歲破)", i.e. the Day Branch clashes with the current Year Branch; that day is unusable.

# Part-5: Date Selection

Not only is it necessary to select the burial date, an appropriate time has also to be selected, down to a 2-hour (120 minutes) slot.

Hour selection is another important step. To be proficient, one really has to study date selection in some detail. As a very rough guide, most "tōng shū" and Chinese calendars will mark the hours of the day in red for auspicious, black for inauspicious, but I would stress this should only be taken as a very rough (almost laughable) guide. In fact it is not uncommon to see "tōng shū" having their red and black ink mixed up. Unfortunately there is no short cut but to learn the subject if one wants to do a good job. It makes a very poor practitioner indeed to have to rely on the colour of the ink to select a good hour!

The "12 Day Officers" formula is a widely used date selection tool, but is by no means the only tool. There are many other systems in use, 2 other popular ones being the "xuán kōng dà guà (玄空大卦)", and the "qí mén dùn jiǎ (奇門遁甲)" systems. Users of these systems claim extraordinary effect, but the systems are complex and difficult to learn.

A date selected by whichever system needs to be personalized for the deceased. This topic is discussed in the next chapter.

# CHAPTER-5.2
## Personalizing a Date

Part-5: Date Selection

## CHAPTER-5.2
### Personalizing a Date

Much like burial plot selection, a selected date has to be personalized for the deceased. Here again there are multiple ways of personalizing a date, but as we have used the sān hè method for tomb orientation earlier in this handbook, we shall confine our discussions to the sān hè method of date personalization here.

By personalization, we mean the selected date has to be compatible with the deceased person's natural inclinations, as determined by his birth Year Pillar. The date has also to be compatible with the tomb, as determined by the "Gold Division" on which the tomb sits (Chp-3.3).

The parameters are:

– nà yīn element of the selected date;

– nà yīn element of the deceased's birth Year Pillar;

– nà yīn element of the tomb Sitting's "Gold Division".

The date's element must "grow" or "prosper" the person's element; the date's element must also "grow" or "prosper" the tomb's element; and the tomb's element must "grow" or "prosper" (or at least does not "counter") the person's element. The person or tomb "countering" the date is acceptable but not the other way round. This tripartite relationship is illustrated in Fig-17.

Part-5: Date Selection

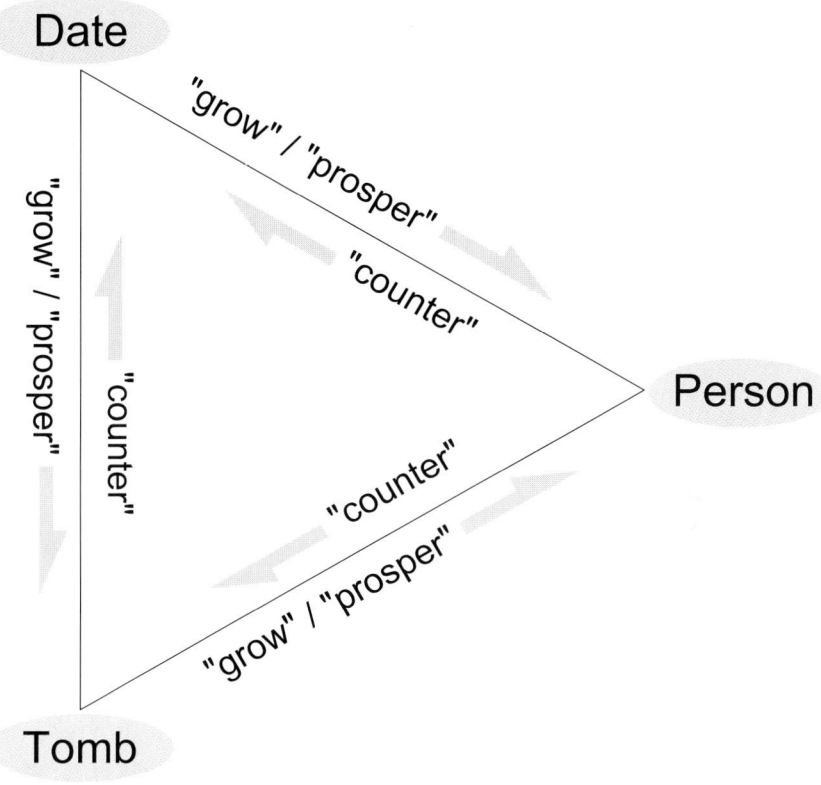

**FIG-17: Date Personalization**

For example, suppose the deceased was born in 甲子 year, nà yīn element Metal; and the tomb sits on 丙戌 "Gold Division", nà yīn element Earth. Let's say a 己酉 Earth day is selected. The date's Earth element "grows" the person's Metal element, and "prospers" the tomb's Earth element. So a 己酉 day would be a perfect match if it also meets the other requirements set out in Chp-5.1

Part-5: Date Selection

The tomb's element in relation to the person's element is already discussed in Chp-3.3.

A Metal day would also be acceptable as the day's Metal "prospers" the person's Metal, and is "grown" by (does not "counter') the tomb's Earth, but this would clearly not be as good as an Earth day.

A Water day is not preferred (but still acceptable at a pinch), as the date's Water would be "grown" by the person's Metal, and "countered" by the tomb's Earth.

A Wood day is unacceptable as Wood "counters" the tomb's Earth.

A Fire day is unacceptable as Fire "counters" the person's Metal.

The elemental interactions work on a host-and-guest relationship. When comparing the date with the person, the person is host and the date guest. When comparing the date with the tomb, the tomb is host and the date guest. The guest should preferably "grow" or "prosper" the host, and in any event must not "counter" the host. A host can "counter" a guest. A host "growing" a guest is not preferred but marginally acceptable. [See Chp-3.3 footnote [13]]

The next chapter discusses certain limitations in the modern setting, and what we can do about it. It will also touch on some of the cultural issues that a modern practitioner is likely to encounter.

# CHAPTER-5.3
## Some Practical Issues

Part-5: Date Selection

## CHAPTER-5.3
### Some Practical Issues

### 1. Limited Window

In the old days, it was fairly common to keep a sealed casket in storage for months or even years waiting for the right date to bury. Today, after the corpse has been removed from the refrigerated morgue, it has to be buried within 5 days. They just don't make caskets like they used to anymore.

So unless the body is kept in the morgue for an extended period, and the death only announced when a suitable date is found, which is hard to accept socially, it means the window for date selection is very narrow. Allowing 1 or 2 days for the wake, the practitioner is left with a 3 or 4-day window. Sometimes there just isn't any suitable date in that window. So what do we do?

Compromise becomes inevitable. The practitioner will just have to pick a date that is the least undesirable, given the limited scope.

Of the "12 Day Officers", "Break" day (Day Branch clashing with Month Branch) is the most severe. A very confident practitioner will sometimes use a "Break" day, but not very often, and only after due consideration. By and large a "Break" day should be avoided. The other nominally unsuitable Day Officers are less severe, and the practitioner may have no choice but to invoke one of them.

Part-5: Date Selection

A Day Branch that clashes with the deceased's Year Branch is another no-no.

Of the unusable days mentioned in Chp-5.1, "Year Breaker" is the least harmful. So if one has little choice, selecting a "Year Breaker" becomes the least undesirable option.

Selecting the right hour for burial will mitigate a compromised day to a degree.

## 2. Tombstone Erection

To compensate for a less-than-favourable burial date, we could select a very good date for erecting the tombstone.

It is customary to wait for 100 days or longer after the burial before the tombstone is erected. The original reason for this 100-day wait was presumably to allow sufficient time for the back-filled earth to settle. As a modern tombstone is usually erected on a reinforced concrete plinth outside the burial pit, and the pit itself is lined with bricks or concrete blocks anyway, earth settlement is no longer an issue, but the custom is usually observed anyway.

The extended interval also gives the practitioner enough leeway to select a really good date for tombstone erection. If the burial was done on a compromised date by necessity, erecting the tombstone on a superior date will compensate for the deficiency to some extent.

This is yet another reason why a tomb layout drawing (Fig-16) is invaluable. After a 3 to 4-month wait, the practitioner could do with a reminder of the original design parameters before he sets the tombstone. The practitioner's presence at this event is mandatory. Do not forget that tombstone alignment is all-important as the tombstone dictates the facing of the entire tomb. Simply relying on the tomb builder's diligence will not do.

It may sound like a simple task but, trust me, setting the desired tombstone facing requires skill. I have personally come across situations in which the behaviour of the luó pán needle defied logical explanation. Such situations make demanding calls on the fēngshuǐ master's experience and judgment.

## 3. Fēngshuǐ & Religion

In ancient times, nobility and the well-to-do have always employed fēngshuǐ masters separately from priests to officiate at a burial. They each performed their own functions, with the fēngshuǐ master setting the orientation and the priest conducting the ceremony.

Later on, probably for economic reasons, the 2 roles were collapsed into one, and the Daoist priest was called upon to be both practitioner and priest. This led to the image of fēngshuǐ taking on religious overtones, especially Daoist traditions, which was most unfortunate. By right classical fēngshuǐ is non-religious. Its association with Daoism was a historical accident, and thankfully, the 2 disciplines have begun to part ways again, as modern fēngshuǐ schools teach classical fēngshuǐ in its original secular and demystified form.

Yet there are some old school practitioners today who still recite prescribed verses or chants during various parts of the burial process, and some clients are led to believe that these chants are part and parcel of fēngshuǐ[19]. Let me state categorically there is no fēngshuǐ basis for such a practice, none whatsoever. The chanting of verses is a Daoist practice, not a fēngshuǐ one. It is evident these verses were colorations acquired in the days when fēngshuǐ and Daoism were casual bedfellows. Modern fēngshuǐ masters do not chant. We leave that to the priests.

[Modern fēngshuǐ masters are more comfortable singing at karaoke joints ☺.]

---

19  Believe it or not, there is even a special verse to be recited each time a luó pán is opened!

Part-5: Date Selection

## 4. Rejection by Certain Faiths

Many Chinese families today have certain family members who embraced the Christian faith while the rest of the family remained culturally Chinese. Some, but not all, Christians have a very jaundiced view of fēngshuǐ. They often object vehemently against fēngshuǐ being applied to the burial of their departed kin, while others in the family may want that.

I have encountered such a situation before. In order to avoid adding stress to an already divided family, I advised my clients to do the following:

- Select a suitable plot according to fēngshuǐ principles;

- Avoid tilting the tombstone. If necessary, tilt the casket alignment instead;

- Design the tomb to impart a neutral or Christian flavour if desired. The appearance of the tomb has little fēngshuǐ significance;

- Omit the "Earth Deity". As mentioned in Chp-4.2, it is not a major issue;

- On the day of burial, the funeral party is requested to take a rest at the reception hall (all modern memorial parks have one) while the casket is carried to the burial pit. The fēngshuǐ practitioner will follow the casket and ensure it is aligned correctly when lowered into the pit;

- Timing is important. The whole exercise will have to be planned carefully so that the casket arrives at the burial site at the appointed time. The funeral party should not be made to wait too long;

- Once the casket is properly lowered, the practitioner leaves the site. The funeral party is then invited to approach the graveside and the priest or pastor takes over for the ceremonial part.

## 5. Re-burial

The idea of exhuming human remains for processing and re-burial may be repugnant to some, but it is part and parcel of yīn house fēngshuǐ. Sometimes re-burial is necessary because the original burial grounds have been delineated for other usage. At other times, a series of misfortunes befalling the deceased's family could suggest that the original burial was defective.

The option for re-burial would then arise. We won't go into the details of exhumation and processing of the remains. That work will be handled by the undertakers. From the fēngshuǐ perspective, the act of re-burial is no different from moving house in the world of the living. In Taiwan, they have even coined the term "auspicious burial (吉葬)" to describe a re-burial exercise.

The bones after being washed are placed into a large urn with the name of the deceased inscribed on the side.[20] A new burial site is found and the urn buried on a selected date. The site and tombstone orientation are decided on the same criteria as for a first time burial, except that accurate alignment of the urn is not required. The urn is simply placed into the pit with the inscription facing the same general direction as the tombstone.

Instead of re-burying the bones, some families prefer to convert the remains into ashes which are then placed in a smaller urn. The rest of the re-burial exercise is the same. Sometimes a unanimous decision to re-bury may be difficult to obtain when the family is large. As always, the job of the practitioner is to advise, leaving the decision to the family.

---

20 Inside the urn, the bones are arranged in an upright foetal position, more or less, with the skull facing the side with the inscription, so that after burial the skull will face outwards.

Part-5: Date Selection

### 6. Recycling the Plot

The question is often asked whether a plot, after exhumation, can be reused for another burial. Strictly speaking, this should not be done. The earth qì in the plot has already been used up, so to speak, i.e. first come first served.

However, in some densely populated territories like Hong Kong where a burial plot can fetch astronomical prices, it is not uncommon to have the remains exhumed after some years for re-burial in an urn packed into a corner of the same plot, and the space vacated is then reused for another member of the family.

In a contest between theory and practicality, we know which side will win. As practitioners, we can only offer our advice if sought.

In Singapore, the government discourages landed burial, and the burial plots offered are not only tiny but also leased for 15 years only. After that period, the remains will have to be exhumed. Whether the old burial grounds will be recycled or used for other purposes, only time will tell. Again practicality overrules theory. From the fēngshuǐ standpoint, it is unlikely Singapore will produce any future emperor! Perhaps reality also supports that view.

In modern China, the preference for landed burial is gaining popularity among the nouveau riche. Some modern memorial parks are built on land that used to be ancient tomb sites. If centuries have passed since the old tombs were abandoned, it is reasonable to argue that the earth has had enough time to replenish its qì, and hence the land becomes usable again.

## End Note

This handbook is intended as a practical guide. Although it does not cover all possible scenarios, the info provided should apply to the vast majority of cases a modern practitioner is likely to encounter in practice.

There are of course extraordinary landforms that call for special consideration. Some of these may indeed contain superior "Meridian Spots (龍眞穴的)", but the chances are pretty remote. To find a usable Meridian Spot requires expert knowledge, endless patience, and tenacious leg work to "walk the Dragons". There is a saying "Nature hides its secrets well".

This handbook sets out to supplement but not replace classical fēngshuǐ texts, for after all classical fēngshuǐ is founded on classical texts and modulated by traditions. To improve his knowledge, the reader is encouraged to read more and take part in group discussions. Some on-line forums are very good sources of information.

However, be aware that textbook knowledge is often ambiguous; traditions may be outdated; whereas the practice of fēngshuǐ is a live art that changes with time and expectations. The success or otherwise of a modern practitioner will depend on his ability to adapt his classical knowledge base to the practical situation on hand, with sensitivity but not slavish submission to age-old traditions.

If this handbook can help to guide the practitioner along this path in however small a way, it will have served its purpose well.

# Appendix-1

## Chinese Characters

Appendix-1: Chinese Characters

## Appendix-1
### Chinese Characters

The following 30 Chinese characters are widely used in this handbook. They need to be learnt for this book to make any sense at all. As a refresher, these characters are listed below with their Romanized pīnyīn versions, and some of the fēngshuǐ attributes associated with the words:

| Chinese character | pīnyīn | fēngshuǐ attributes |
|---|---|---|
| **10 Heavenly Stems:** | | |
| 甲 | jiǎ | yáng Wood |
| 乙 | yǐ | yīn Wood |
| 丙 | bǐng | yáng Fire |
| 丁 | dīng | yīn Fire |
| 戊 | wù | yáng Earth |
| 己 | jǐ | yīn Earth |
| 庚 | gēng | yáng Metal |
| 辛 | xīn | yīn Metal |
| 壬 | rén | yáng Water |
| 癸 | guǐ | yīn Water |

The words describe the 5 elements of Chinese Metaphysics, each element subdivided into its yīn and yáng forms, making up 10 variables.

# Appendix-1: Chinese Characters

| Chinese character | pīnyīn | fēngshuǐ attributes |
|---|---|---|
| **12 Earthly Branches:** | | |
| 子 | zǐ | "Rat" |
| 丑 | chǒu | "Ox" |
| 寅 | yín | "Tiger" |
| 卯 | mǎo | "Rabbit" |
| 辰 | chén | "Dragon" |
| 巳 | sì | "Snake" |
| 午 | wǔ | "Horse" |
| 未 | wèi | "Goat" |
| 申 | shēn | "Monkey" |
| 酉 | yǒu | "Rooster" |
| 戌 | xū | "Dog" |
| 亥 | hài | "Pig" |

The animal names are popular aliases, but really quite meaningless. The 12 words actually describe the 12 segments of the sky through which the ecliptic passes, i.e. a heavenly feature, not unlike the 12 "Houses" of Western Astrology. The guy who coined the term "*Earthly* Branches" obviously had an odd sense of humour.

## Appendix-1: Chinese Characters

| Chinese character | pīnyīn | Symbol | fēngshuǐ attributes |
|---|---|---|---|
| **8 Trigrams:** | | | |
| 乾 | qián | ☰ | Heaven; Northwest; father |
| 兌 | duì | ☱ | Marsh; West; youngest daughter |
| 離 | lí | ☲ | Fire; South; middle daughter |
| 震 | zhèn | ☳ | Thunder; East; eldest son |
| 巽 | xùn | ☴ | Wind; Southeast; eldest daughter |
| 坎 | kǎn | ☵ | Water; North; middle son |
| 艮 | gèn | ☶ | Mountain; Northeast; youngest son |
| 坤 | kūn | ☷ | Earth; Southwest; mother |

The 8 Trigrams, or "guà (卦)", are fundamental building blocks of Chinese Metaphysics. Ancient philosophers explained all objects and events, natural or man-made, in terms of these 8 variables.

# Appendix-2

## Human Plate 5 Elements

## Appendix-2
### Human Plate 5 Elements

In the main body of the handbook, I have deliberately steered clear of theoretical discussions, but to satisfy the curiosity of the more inquisitive readers, I thought I would expand a little on the "Human Plate 5 Elements (HP5E)" in this Appendix. The topic was introduced in Chp-2.5

The Human Plate of the sān hè luó pán, as well as the HP5E were inventions of the famous Sòng Dynasty (960~1276 CE) fēngshuǐ master, Lài BùYī (賴布衣). He led a very eventful, and by some accounts a rather colourful life. Master Lài was an accomplished astronomer, as evidenced by his signature treatise "Advancing Officer Scrolls (催官篇)", in which he related the 24 Mountains of the luó pán to stars in the heavens, but that's another story.

His invention of the Human Plate was an attempt to relate earthbound mountains to the heavenly stars, and in particular the 28-Constellations. In modern astronomical language, these "Constellations" are in fact asterisms (arbitrary groupings of stars) in a band through which the ecliptic (perceived path of the sun) and the planets pass. They are very similar in concept to the Western Zodiac, and indeed many of the stars in the 28-Constellations are also featured in the Zodiac.

To more or less line up the 24-Mountains of the luó pán with the 28-Constellations, Master Lài had to rotate the 24-Mountains Earth Plate counter-clockwise by 7½°. This gave rise to what we now call the Human Plate.

# Appendix-2: Human Plate 5 Elements

Having created his new 24-Mountains plate, Master Lái then assigned an element to each of the Mountains on this plate. Not surprisingly, these elements should reflect the elements of the 28-Constellations, and they are different from the standard 5 elements normally associated with the 24-Mountains of the Earth Plate.

As to how the 28-Constellations got their elements, it's a long story that I will let pass, except to say that the elements in this case are associated with the 5 visible planets of our solar system plus the sun and the moon. They are "Wood (木)" of the planet Jupiter; "Metal (金)" of Venus; "Earth (土)" of Saturn; "Sun (日)"; "Moon (月)"; "Fire (火)" of Mars; and "Water (水)" of Mercury.

Evidently these 7 elements of the Constellations are not the same as the 5 elements of Chinese Metaphysics. Many scholars argued that the 28-Constellations were foreign imports from ancient Babylonia, Persia and India; but through the ages they were assimilated into Chinese Metaphysics.

In force fitting the elements of the Constellations into the 24-Mountains of the Human Plate, Master Lái did some tweaking:

– "Sun" and "Moon" were both regarded as being of Fire element. This is peculiar to the HP5E. In some other fēngshuǐ applications, "Sun" is Fire but "Moon" is Water.

– Each of the 24-Mountains has a fixed width (15°), but the Constellations vary in angular spreads between ½° and 30°. Moreover there are 28 Constellations but only 24 Mountains. Some of the Mountains cover more than one Constellation, in which case the brightest star was used to determine the Constellation of reference.

Appendix-2: Human Plate 5 Elements

In this way, each of the 24-Mountain on the Human Plate was assigned the element of its reference Constellation, and a new distribution of the 5 elements, called HP5E, was born.

The table below compares the HP5E with their respective Constellations. Please note it is the Human Plate 24-Mountains (人盤中針) that we are using; and the Constellations are read off the so-called "old" 28-Constellations plate that was drawn up around 1205 CE (開禧二十八宿盤).

| HP 24-Mountains | HP 5 Elements | Constellations (Elements) |
|---|---|---|
| 亥 | Water | 壁 Wall (Water) |
| 壬 | Fire | 室 Encampment (Fire) |
| 子 | Fire | 危 Rooftop (Water) |
| 癸 | Earth | 虛 Emptiness (Sun); 女 Girl (Earth) |
| 丑 | Metal | 女 Girl (Earth); 牛 Ox (Metal) |
| 艮 | Wood | 斗 Dipper (Wood) |
| 寅 | Water | 斗 Dipper (Wood); 箕 Winnowing Basket (Water) |
| 甲 | Fire | 尾 Tail (Fire) |
| 卯 | Fire | 心 Heart (Moon); 房 Room (Sun) |
| 乙 | Earth | 氐 Root (Earth) |

## Appendix-2: Human Plate 5 Elements

| HP 24-Mountains | HP 5 Elements | Constellations (Elements) |
|---|---|---|
| 辰 | Metal | 亢 Neck (Metal); 角 Horn (Wood) |
| 巽 | Wood | 角 Horn (Wood) |
| 巳 | Water | 軫 Chariot (Water); 翼 Wings (Fire) |
| 丙 | Fire | 翼 Wings (Fire) |
| 午 | Fire | 張 Extended Net (Moon) |
| 丁 | Earth | 星 Star (Sun); 柳 Willow (Earth) |
| 未 | Metal | 柳 Willow (Earth); 鬼 Ghosts (Metal) |
| 坤 | Wood | 井 Well (Wood) |
| 申 | Water | 井 Well (Wood); 参 3 Stars (Water) |
| 庚 | Fire | 觜 Turtle Beak (Fire); 畢 Net (Moon) |
| 酉 | Fire | 昴 Hairy Head (Sun) |
| 辛 | Earth | 胃 Stomach (Earth) |
| 戌 | Metal | 婁 Bond (Metal) |
| 乾 | Wood | 奎 Legs (Wood) |

The yīn House Handbook

# Appendix-2: Human Plate 5 Elements

Note that the Mountains diametrically opposite each other have the same HP5E.

As explained in Chp-2.5, the Human Plate and HP5E are used to evaluate Embraces, which are the hills or tall structures visible from the tomb.

For example, a hill located at 亥 on the Human Plate is deemed to be associated with the Constellation "Wall" in the heavens, and will partake of the latter's Water element. This element is then compared with the HP5E of the tomb's Sitting Mountain. The method of comparison and the conclusions drawn are described in Chp-2.5

It sounds simple enough, but there is a fly-in-the-ointment...

Master Lài lived in the early part of the 12th Century, about 900 years ago. The stars that he observed are no longer to be found at the same positions today. There is an astronomical phenomenon called "Precession of the Equinoxes" that effectively moves the stars about 1° to the West every 72 years, as observed from the earth. [The stars don't actually move. It's the rotational axis of the earth that moves. In everyday language, the earth wobbles slightly about its axis.]

In 900 years the stars would have moved about 12.5°, which means some of the stars will have moved into an adjacent Mountain compared with the time when Master Lài observed the heavens.

Some masters argue that for Master Lài's method to continue giving good results, an up-to-date star chart should be used, and the HP5E revisited accordingly.

## Appendix-2: Human Plate 5 Elements

Other masters take a different view. They argue that a typical hill has been around for millions of years, whereas Precession comes full cycle every 26,000 years or so. In other words, a hill would have gone through numerous Precession cycles from its formation to the present time. Master Lài merely established a computational method, and the point in time at which the method was established is really immaterial.

The scholars take pleasure in debate but most practitioners, being practical people, tend to work with the Human Plate just as Master Lài had designed it.

# Appendix-3

nà yīn Elements

## Appendix-3
### nà yīn Elements

Several of the techniques described in the handbook invoked an entity called nà yīn elements (納音五行). In line with the book's emphasis on practice over theory, I did not bother to explain the concept of nà yīn in the main text, but thought I should do so in this Appendix, in case some readers wish to know.

All students of fēngshuǐ, at some stage or other of their studies, would have been perplexed by nà yīn elements. The following questions spring readily to mind:

– What are they?
– How are they derived?
– Why the strange names?
– What are they used for?

The mystery would be effectively unveiled by answering these questions. Let me take them one at a time:

# Appendix-3: nà yīn Elements

## 1. What are nà yīn elements?

The term "nà yīn" translated ad verbatim means "to take in a tone". So are nà yīn elements tones of different pitches (frequencies)? Not that I know of, although that should make an interesting topic for research.

To put it simply, nà yīn elements are, well, just elements. Some call them tonal elements. They are a sub-set of the 5 standard elements, Wood/Fire/Earth/Metal/Water, that form the backbone of all Chinese Metaphysics.

At the entry level, fēngshuǐ students are taught that the 10 Heavenly Stems are each associated with an element, and so are the 12 Earthly Branches and the 8 Trigrams. These are called "Basic 5 Elements (正五行)", and they are summarized in the following table:

| 10 Heavenly Stems | | 12 Earthly Branches | | 8 Trigrams | |
|---|---|---|---|---|---|
| 甲 | Wood | 子 | Water | 乾 | Metal |
| 乙 | Wood | 丑 | Earth | 兌 | Metal |
| 丙 | Fire | 寅 | Wood | 離 | Fire |
| 丁 | Fire | 卯 | Wood | 震 | Wood |
| 戊 | Earth | 辰 | Earth | 巽 | Wood |
| 己 | Earth | 巳 | Fire | 坎 | Water |
| 庚 | Metal | 午 | Fire | 艮 | Earth |
| 辛 | Metal | 未 | Earth | 坤 | Earth |
| 壬 | Water | 申 | Metal | | |
| 癸 | Water | 酉 | Metal | | |
| | | 戌 | Earth | | |
| | | 亥 | Water | | |

## Appendix-3: nà yīn Elements

But that is not the end of the story. For example, students at the intermediate level are introduced to the "Paired-mountains 5 Elements (雙山五行)", and the "Human Plate 5 Elements (中針五行)". These are sub-sets made up of the same 5 elements Wood/Fire/Earth/Metal/Water, but they are distributed amongst the Heavenly Stems, Earthly Branches and Trigrams in different ways.

Then there are 60 values each made up of a Stem and a Branch, commonly called the 60 "jiǎ zǐ". Each of these values is assigned an element that may not be the same as the basic element of its constituent Stem or Branch. This new sub-set is called nà yīn elements, and the 60 values and their respective elements are listed below:

| 甲子, 乙丑 Metal | 甲戌, 乙亥 Fire | 甲申, 乙酉 Water |
|---|---|---|
| 丙寅, 丁卯 Fire | 丙子, 丁丑 Water | 丙戌, 丁亥 Earth |
| 戊辰, 己巳 Wood | 戊寅, 己卯 Earth | 戊子, 己丑 Fire |
| 庚午, 丁未 Earth | 庚辰, 辛巳 Metal | 庚寅, 辛卯 Wood |
| 壬申, 癸酉 Metal | 壬午, 癸未 Wood | 壬辰, 癸巳 Water |
| 甲午, 乙未 Metal | 甲辰, 乙巳 Fire | 甲寅, 乙卯 Water |
| 丙申, 丁酉 Fire | 丙午, 丁未 Water | 丙辰, 丁巳 Earth |
| 戊戌, 己亥 Wood | 戊申, 己酉 Earth | 戊午, 己未 Fire |
| 庚子, 辛丑 Earth | 庚戌, 辛亥 Metal | 庚申, 辛酉 Wood |
| 壬寅, 癸卯 Metal | 壬子, 癸丑 Wood | 壬戌, 癸亥 Water |

But why the seemingly haphazard order, and what has it got to do with tones? The answers will come to light in the following section.

# Appendix-3: nà yīn Elements

## 2. How are nà yīn elements derived?

Let us digress for a moment and look at the structure of Chinese classical music. The reason for this digression will become clear shortly.

Chinese classical music has 12 scales that are named "黃鐘 (huáng zhōng)", "大呂 (dà lǚ)", "太簇 (tài cù)", "夾鐘 (jiá zhōng)", "姑洗 (gū xǐ)", "仲呂 (zhòng lǚ)" "蕤賓 (ruí bīn)", "林鐘 (lín zhōng)", "夷則 (yí zé)", "南呂 (nán lǚ)", "無射 (wú shè)" and "應鐘 (yìng zhōng)", respectively. Half of them (the odd numbered ones) are called "律 (lǜ)", and the other half (even numbered) called "呂 (lǚ)". These outrageous names are meaningless to all but serious musicians. [For readers who want to know more, there are several websites that provide a deeper insight, in English. Just google "Chinese music" and have fun!]

For the rest of us, the key point is that half are of one group (lǜ); the other half of another but complementary group (lǚ). In Metaphysical language, that would be yáng and yīn.

In addition, each scale is pentatonic, meaning it contains 5 notes, unlike 7 in the Western diatonic scale. The 5 notes are named "宮 (gōng)", "商 (shāng)", "角 (jué)", "徵 (zhǐ)" and "羽 (yǔ)" from low to high, which roughly correspond to do, re, mi, so, la in the Western scale. The notes fa and si are absent in the Chinese scale.

These 5 notes are analogous to the 5 elements of Chinese Metaphysics: gōng takes on the element Earth; shāng Metal; jué Wood; zhǐ Fire; yuě Water.

# Appendix-3: nà yīn Elements

The 12 scales and 5 notes together give us 60 tones. These are grouped into 30 pairs of complementary tones.

[Please forgive me if I used the words "scale", "note" and "tone" incorrectly, for I am no musician by any stretch of the imagination ☹]

Now look at our familiar 60 "jiǎ zǐ". If the 60 values are arranged into 30 pairs (1 yáng 1 yīn) and each pair is assigned an element, we have created a sub-set of 30 entities that have a close parallel in musical tones. That was how the idea of "nà yīn", meaning "to take in a tone", took root.

But what about the order of the elements? They appear to be haphazard but are in reality quite regimented, albeit in a rather complex way:

a. The 1st rule states that the order of the nà yīn elements shall be Metal → Fire → Wood → Water → Earth. That completes one cycle. The next cycle starts all over again with Metal.

This order is of course very different from the natural order of the basic 5 elements, which is Wood → Fire → Earth → Metal → Water. Scholars have ventured several explanations. I find the following 2 explanations more credible than the others:

## Appendix-3: nà yīn Elements

– The following diagram depicts the Early Heaven arrangement of the 8 Trigrams and their respective elements:

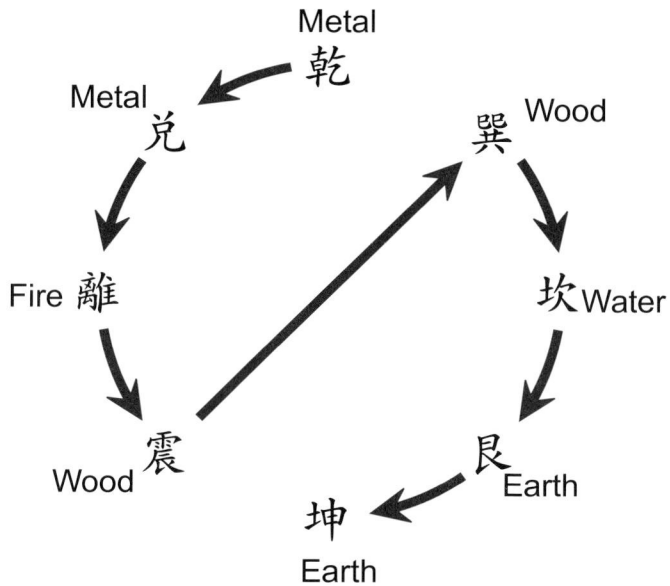

**Fig-A3.1: Order of nà yīn elements**

乾 represents heaven and the ultimate yáng. Its element is Metal. It is therefore not surprising that the order should start with Metal.

The natural progression of the Early Heaven 8 Trigrams is: 乾 (Metal) → 兌 (Metal) → 離 (Fire) → 震 (Wood) → 巽 (Wood) → 坎 (Water) → 艮 (Earth) → 坤 (Earth), as shown in Fig-A3.1

坤 represents the earth and the ultimate yīn. Its position at the tail end is in keeping with the earth's yielding and magnanimous nature.

## Appendix-3: nà yīn Elements

Think of it this way: it's the male (yáng) that makes the first move, but the female (yīn) ends up holding the baby [with apologies to the feminists] ☺

The nà yīn elements follow this natural order of the universe.

– Whereas the natural order of the basic 5 elements observes the "Growth Cycle", i.e. Wood → Fire → Earth → Metal → Water, the nà yīn elements observe an "Applications Cycle".

For Metal to become useful, it has to be forged by Fire. Hence Metal is followed by Fire.

A fundamental property of Fire is to be bright and attractive. To achieve this, Fire needs to be sustained by Wood. Hence Fire is followed by Wood.

Wood symbolizes growth. Water is essential for Wood to grow. Hence Wood is followed by Water.

Water only becomes useful if it is constrained and guided by Earth. Hence Water is followed by Earth.

Earth becomes valuable if it contains Metal. Hence Earth is followed by Metal… and the cycle repeats itself ad infinitum.

Appendix-3: nà yīn Elements

b. The 2nd rule says "Take the same kind as one's wife; skip 8 to beget a son (同類娶妻, 隔八生子)". This rule too has musical origins, but the mechanics are too complicated to be explained here. [A fair description is given in the bā zì encyclopedia "三命通會 (sān mìng tōng huì)."]

What it means is that if 2 adjacent Stems are of the same (basic) element, they are treated as a husband-and-wife pair, and they share the same nà yīn element. Furthermore the next item in the sequence is not the "jiǎ zǐ" value that immediately follows, but the one 8 places down the line.

The sequence naturally starts from 甲子 (1st Heavenly Stem + 1st Earthly Branch). This is followed by 乙丑. As 甲 and 乙 are both of the same basic element Wood, 乙丑 becomes the wife of 甲子 and the 2 of them share the same nà yīn element. Rule #1 says that should be Metal.

The next generation is not 丙寅, as one may have expected, but is instead the item in 8th place after 甲子. That turns out to be 壬申. So 壬申 becomes the son of 甲子/乙丑, and takes 癸酉 as his wife. The next generation after that is the item in 8th place after 壬申, which turns out to be 庚辰. So 庚辰 becomes the son of 壬申/癸酉 and takes 辛巳 as his wife.

The first 3 pairs in the new sequence are therefore: 甲子/乙丑 → 壬申/癸酉 → 庚辰/辛巳, and all of them carry the nà yīn element Metal.

By the same logical manoeuvre, the following 3 pairs in the new sequence are: 戊子/己丑 → 丙申/丁酉 → 甲辰/乙巳, but their nà yīn element is no longer Metal. It has become Fire instead.

## Appendix-3: nà yīn Elements

Proceeding the same way, the next 3 pairs are 壬子/癸丑 → 庚申/辛酉 → 戊辰/癸巳, but their nà yīn element has changed to Wood.

The 3 pairs following that are 丙子/丁丑 → 甲申/乙酉 → 壬辰/癸巳. In their case, the nà yīn element is Water.

And the 3 pairs after that are 庚子/辛丑 → 戊申/己酉 → 丙辰/丁巳, and their nà yīn element is Earth.

We have now arrived at the midway point, having covered 30 of the 60 "jiǎ zǐ" values, and having gone one round with the 5 elements: Metal, Fire, Wood, Water and Earth.

The 2nd part of the sequence starts with 甲午, and the story is repeated exactly as before. In other words, the first 3 pairs in the 2nd part are 甲午/乙未 → 壬寅/癸卯 → 庚戌/辛亥, and their nà yīn element reverts to Metal; … and so on. That should take us to the 30th pair of "jiǎ zǐ" values and the end of the sequence.

The following table lists all the 60 "jiǎ zǐ" (in 30 pairs) and their respective nà yīn elements in the genealogical sequence, which is clearly not the same as the natural sequence stated in section-1 above.

| #1 甲子/乙丑 Metal | #2 壬申/癸酉 Metal | #3 庚辰/辛巳 Metal |
|---|---|---|
| 丙寅… | 甲戌… | 壬午… |
| 戊辰… | 丙子… | 甲申… |
| 庚午… | 戊寅… | 丙戌… |
| #4 戊子/己丑 Fire | #5 丙申/丁酉 Fire | #6 甲辰/乙巳 Fire |
| 庚… | 戊… | 丙… |
| 壬… | 庚… | 戊… |
| 甲… | 壬… | 庚… |

# Appendix-3: nà yīn Elements

| #7 壬子/癸丑 Wood | #8 庚申/辛酉 Wood | #9 戊辰/己巳 Wood |
| --- | --- | --- |
| 甲… | 壬… | 庚… |
| 丙… | 甲… | 壬… |
| 戊… | 丙… | 甲… |
| #10 丙子/丁丑 Water | #11 甲申/乙酉 Water | #12 壬辰/癸巳 Water |
| 戊… | 丙… | 甲… |
| 庚… | 戊… | 丙… |
| 壬… | 庚… | 戊… |
| #13 庚子/辛丑 Earth | #14 戊申/己酉 Earth | #15 丙辰/丁巳 Earth |
| 壬… | 庚… | 戊… |
| 甲… | 壬… | 庚… |
| 丙… | 甲… | 壬… |
| #16 甲午/乙末 Metal | #17 壬寅/癸卯 Metal | #18 庚戌/辛亥 Metal |
| 丙… | 甲… | 壬… |
| 戊… | 丙… | 甲… |
| 庚… | 戊… | 丙… |
| #19 戊午/己末 Fire | #20 丙寅/丁卯 Fire | #21 甲戌/乙亥 Fire |
| 庚… | 戊… | 丙… |
| 壬… | 庚… | 戊… |
| 甲… | 壬… | 庚… |
| #22 壬午/癸末 Wood | #23 庚寅/辛卯 Wood | #24 戊戌/己亥 Wood |
| 甲… | 壬… | 庚… |
| 丙… | 甲… | 壬… |
| 戊… | 丙… | 甲… |

## Appendix-3: nà yīn Elements

| #25 丙午/丁未 Water | #26 甲寅/乙卯 Water | #27 壬戌/癸亥 Water |
|---|---|---|
| 戊… | 丙… | 甲… |
| 庚… | 戊… | 丙… |
| 壬… | 庚… | 戊… |
| #28 庚午/辛未 Earth | #29 戊寅/己卯 Earth | #30 丙戌/丁亥 Earth |
| 壬… | 庚… | 戊… |
| 甲… | 壬… | 庚… |
| 丙… | 甲… | 壬… |

Note that each nà yīn element is applied 3 times before it changes. There is a reason for this. The observant reader would have noticed that the 1st occurrence is always at the Branch 子 or 午; the 2nd occurrence is at 申 or 寅; and the 3rd occurrence at 辰 or 戌.

子 and 午 are called "Middle (仲)" Branches; 申 and 寅 are "Beginning (孟)" Branches; and 辰 and 戌 are "End of Season (季)" Branches. Having visited all 3 Branches in a set (子/申/辰 or 午/寅/戌), the element has completed a cycle, and the next element takes over in the subsequent generation.

**FAQ:** Given any "jiǎ zǐ" value, is there a way to find its nà yīn element without having to refer to tables?

There are in fact several ways. My favourite is described below:

First assign the 5 elements to the 5 digits on one hand (usually the left hand), and assign the 10 Heavenly Stems to the same 5 digits, as shown in Fig-A3.2a.

Appendix-3: nà yīn Elements

Next assign the 12 Earthly Branches to the mounds of the fingers, together with the numerals 1, 2, and 3, as shown in Fig-A3.2b.

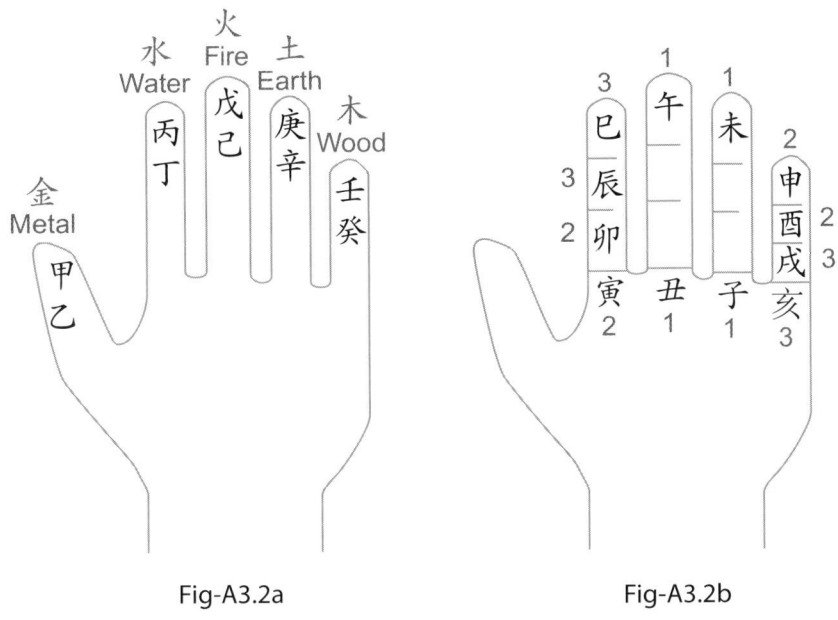

Fig-A3.2a  Fig-A3.2b

**FIG-A3.2: Finding nà yīn Elements**

Follow the steps outlined below:

1. For a given "jiǎ zǐ" value, locate the Earthly Branch in Fig-A3.2b, and take note of the associated numeral;

   eg. for 丙辰, locate 辰 in Fig-A3.2b. Associated numeral is 3.

2. Locate the Heavenly Stem in Fig-A3.2a;

   eg. 丙 is located on the index finger.

## Appendix-3: nà yīn Elements

3. Start counting clockwise from this location, starting with 1, and stopping at the numeral noted in step-1 above. If the counting goes past the little finger, loop back to the thumb;

   eg. index finger =1, middle finger = 2, ring finger = 3. Stop at 3.

4. Look up Fig-A3.2a for the element assigned to the finger at which the counting stopped. That's the required "nà yīn element".

   eg. Counting stopped at ring finger. Element assigned to the ring finger is Earth. Hence the "nà yīn element" for 丙辰 is Earth.

Another example to find the "nà yīn element" for 癸酉:

酉 is associated with numeral 2;
癸 is on the little finger;
Start counting: little finger = 1, thumb = 2. Stop at 2;
Element assigned to the thumb is Metal;
"nà yīn element" for 癸酉 is Metal.

With a little practice, this method provides an easy means to find the "nà yīn element" of any given "jiǎ zǐ" value, without having to refer to tables. Besides, counting one's fingers this way is cool ☺

Appendix-3: nà yīn Elements

### 3. Why the strange names?

Ready for more? As mentioned in the previous section, each of the 5 elements occurs 6 times in the sequence. The 6 versions of Metal are different from one another; and likewise for Fire, Wood, Water and Earth. There are altogether 30 different nà yīn elements, and each nà yīn element is given a unique name – talking about splitting hairs!

Ask any fēngshuǐ master, and he is unlikely to be able to tell you much about these unique and unusual names. Very few masters bother, but my curiosity led me to research the classics. The answers may not be universally accepted, some are decidedly dodgy, but at least they tried to put some rationality behind these strange names.

The following table lists the 30 nà yīn elements, each bearing its unique name, and a plausible rationale for that name: [ref. "Book of Unifying Times and Discerning Dimensions (協紀辨方書)" and others]

## Appendix-3: nà yīn Elements

| "jiǎ zǐ" values | nà yīn element | Rationale |
|---|---|---|
| 甲子, 乙丑 | Metal in the sea 海中金 | The Metal is located at 子 and 丑 where Water is strong and Metal is at its "Dead" and "Grave" phases - hence the description of submerged metal. |
| 丙寅, 丁卯 | Fire of the furnace 爐中火 | Fire passes through 寅 and 卯 where Wood is vibrant. The fire is being fed by wood - hence the description of a furnace. |
| 戊辰, 己巳 | Wood of the forest 大林木 | Wood has arrived at 辰 and 巳, at which time the Wood is fully grown and supported by plentiful earth and sunlight. Hence the wood has grown into a dense forest. |
| 庚午, 丁未 | Roadside Earth 路旁土 | At 午 and 未 the Earth is dried out. It no longer supports the growth of plants, much like the earth at the roadside. |
| 壬申, 癸酉 | Sword Metal 劍鋒金 | At 申 and 酉, Metal has reached its peak, and is likened to metal at the tip of a sword. |

# Appendix-3: nà yīn Elements

| "jiǎ zǐ" values | nà yīn element | Rationale |
|---|---|---|
| 甲戌, 乙亥 | Forest Fire 山頭火 | At 戌 and 亥, Fire is at its "Grave" and "Extinct" phases. It is likened to the ending stage of a forest fire when the fire is reduced to ambers but still smoldering beneath the surface. |
| 丙子, 丁丑 | Water of the creek 澗下水 | Water is "Prosperous" at 子, but "Weakens" at 丑. It doesn't have the power of a large river, but is lively enough, rather like the waters of mountain creeks. [Personally I don't buy this explanation, but it's in the books.] |
| 戊寅, 己卯 | Fortress Earth 城頭土 | Earth is at 寅 and 卯 where Wood is vibrant. Although Earth is countered by Wood, 寅 is located at the Trigram 艮 which is also Earth, and 卯 represents herbaceous plants that hold the earth together more than loosens it. Hence the earth builds up into a position of strength, and is likened to a fortress. |
| 庚辰, 辛巳 | Wax Metal 白蠟金 | Metal is "Nurtured" at 辰, and "Grows" at 巳. The metal is at an infancy stage and hasn't quite taken shape yet – hence the description of wax. In fact "wax metal" originally referred to soft metals like lead and tin. |
| 壬午, 癸未 | Willow Wood 楊柳木 | Wood is "Dead" at 午 and enters "Grave" at 未. Although Water in the Stems will try to grow it, the wood is nevertheless weak and lacks rigidity, like a willow tree. |

## Appendix-3: nà yīn Elements

| "jiǎ zǐ" values | nà yīn element | Rationale |
|---|---|---|
| 甲申, 乙酉 | Well Water 井泉水 | Water goes through its "Growth" and "Bath" phases at 申 and 酉 respectively. At its infancy, the flow is not copious, and is likened to the underground water that finds its way into a well. |
| 丙戌, 丁亥 | Rooftop Earth 屋上土 | The Fire Stems 丙 and 丁 grow Earth, but the Earth is located at 戌 and 亥, the so-called "Heaven's Gate". Hence this earth is elevated from ground level, and is likened to roof tiles, which are of course made of earth. |
| 戊子, 己丑 | Thunderbolt Fire 霹靂火 | The Fire is located at 子 and 丑. 子 is the territory of Water. Hence the fire is thought to be rising out of the water, and that in turn conjures up the image of a legendary dragon rising from the waves spitting fire. Such was the imagery used to explain a thunderbolt in ancient times. [Invoking this image in the present context is, to my mind, rather stretched. Couldn't our ancient masters have come up with something more credible?] |
| 庚寅, 辛卯 | Pine Wood 松柏木 | Wood at 寅 and 卯 is at the height of timeliness. 寅 is the "Officer" phase of Wood, and 卯 is "Prosperous". Pine wood has a special place in Chinese culture. Most structural timber and furniture items were made out of pine wood in the old days, and in addition, the pine tree stood as a symbol of strength and uprightness. It is evergreen even in the coldest winter. The pine tree is thus a most appropriate image for Wood at its prime. |
| 壬辰, 癸巳 | Perpetual Water flow 長流水 | 辰 is the "Grave (Storage)" of water; whereas 巳 is the "Growth" of Metal that in turn produces Water. Under such conditions, the water will never dry up – hence the description of perpetual flow. |

## Appendix-3: nà yīn Elements

| "jiǎ zǐ" values | nà yīn element | Rationale |
|---|---|---|
| 甲午, 乙未 | Granular Metal 砂石金 | Fire "Prospers" at 午 and "Weakens" at 未. When Fire roars, Metal cringes. When Fire weakens, Metal gradually recovers. At 午 and 未, Metal barely takes shape – hence the description of granular metal, i.e. metal that has yet to be converted from its ore state, and is not very useful. |
| 丙申, 丁酉 | Fire below the hills 山下火 | The term actually describes a sunset scene where the sun (Fire) gradually sinks below the distant hills, and the sun's heat and radiance slowly diminish. In Metaphysical language, Fire is "Sick" at 申 and "Dead" at 酉. |
| 戊戌, 己亥 | Flatland Wood 平地木 | 戌 represents the wilderness, and 亥 is the "Growth" of Wood. Vegetation that grows in the wilderness is usually unkempt and does not produce quality timber. |
| 庚子, 辛丑 | Earth on the wall 壁上土 | 子 is the territory of Water, and 丑 is wet Earth. Excessive water turns the earth into a mortar paste that can be used to cement a brick or stone wall. |
| 壬寅, 癸卯 | Foil Metal 金箔金 | Wood is strong at 寅 and 卯. When Wood is strong, Metal is ineffective. Moreover Metal is "Extinct" at 寅 and just "Conceived" at 卯. The metal is very fragile, like metal foil. |

## Appendix-3: nà yīn Elements

| "jiǎ zǐ" values | nà yīn element | Rationale |
|---|---|---|
| 甲辰, 乙巳 | Fire of a perpetually lighted lamp 覆燈火 | 辰 is at the transition between spring and summer, and 巳 is early summer. Moreover there is Wood from the Stems to feed the fire. Hence the fire will continue to burn, but is not overbearing as it is still late spring/early summer. The description refers to an oil lamp at the altar that is kept burning all the time. |
| 丙午, 丁未 | Heavenly river Water 天河水 | The Stems 丙 and 丁 are Fire. 午 is also Fire territory. Yet the nà yīn element is Water. The ancients thought that water originating from fire could only mean a river in the heavens. "Heavenly river" is a term used to describe the Milky Way, the galaxy in which our sun is one of the stars. |
| 戊申, 己酉 | Massive Earth on the move 大驛土 | 申 is part of the Trigram 坤 – mother Earth. 酉 is of the Trigram 兌 – a marsh. The Stems 戊 and 己 are Earth. The element Earth in this instance is clearly not a thin crust of floating soil, but a massive amount of earth on the move. Alternatively it could be interpreted as a major road that carries heavy traffic volumes. |
| 庚戌, 辛亥 | Jewelry Metal 釵釧金 | Metal "Weakens" at 戌, and is "Sick" at 亥. The metal is no longer suitable for use as a weapon or tool, but can still be made into attractive jewelry. |
| 壬子, 癸丑 | Wood of the mulberry tree 桑柘木 | 子 is the territory of Water, which promotes the growth of Wood, but there is also hidden Metal in 丑. The image is therefore one of mulberry trees where the young leaves are cut to feed the silk worms. |

# Appendix-3: nà yīn Elements

| "jiǎ zǐ" values | nà yīn element | Rationale |
|---|---|---|
| 甲寅, 乙卯 | Water of a large stream 大溪水 | 寅 is located at the northeast, and 卯 at the east. In China, the major rivers flow from west to east. So water flowing eastward is regarded as a natural flow that will be joined by other streams along the way, gradually turning it into a large stream or river. [Here again I think the explanation is rather stretched.] |
| 丙辰, 丁巳 | Sandy Earth 沙中土 | Earth enters "Grave" at 辰, and becomes "Extinct" at 巳. [Note that Earth is treated like Water in this case.] But at the same time Fire in the Stems is rising, thereby having the capacity to grow more earth. The term sandy earth describes earth that lacks strength but is not totally dysfunctional. |
| 戊午, 己未 | Fire of the sun 天上火 | Fire is "Prosperous" at 午. Although it "Weakens" at 未, there is hidden Wood in 未 to sustain the fire. The image is that of the midday sun: hot and fiercely radiant. |
| 庚申, 辛酉 | Pomegranate Wood 石榴木 | 申 and 酉 are autumn months. Most plants would have started to wilt, but the pomegranate tree still bears fruit. It is therefore seen as an apt description of Wood that stands up to the shrillness of autumn. |
| 壬戌, 癸亥 | Ocean Water 大海水 | Water enters the "Youth" phase at 戌, and "Officer" phase at 亥, growing from strength to strength. Moreover, 亥 also stands for voluminous water. The Stems 壬 and 癸 are also Water. All in all, there is a deluge of water – hence the description of an ocean. |

## Appendix-3: nà yīn Elements

In some applications, the unique name gives a nà yīn element certain unique attributes. For example, "Metal in the sea" can hardly be countered by Fire; and Water cannot possibly put out "Thunderbolt Fire".

However, such explanations are seldom used in fēngshuǐ applications. They are more relevant to destiny analysis.

Do we need to memorize the 30 names? The answer is an emphatic "No!" Didn't I tell you it's only a mental exercise born of curiosity? ☺ One doesn't have to go to that extent to use nà yīn elements.

Appendix-3: nà yīn Elements

## 4. What are nà yīn elements used for?

In the handbook, we have seen how nà yīn elements are used when we discussed "Gold Divisions" (Chp-3.3), and again when we selected a date for burial (Chp-5.2).

In fact nà yīn elements have a much wider use than that. Whenever "jiǎ zǐ" values are encountered in sān hè fēngshuǐ, it is more than likely that their nà yīn elements will be invoked.

In the sān hè luó pán, the "72 Dragons" plate, "60 Dragons" plates, and the "120 Dragons" plates all feature "jiǎ zǐ" values. The formulae that relate to these plates will invariably make use of nà yīn elements. It is just that some schools use them more intensively than others.

Apart from fēngshuǐ applications, nà yīn elements are also used in bā zì destiny analysis, in one of its variants.

This Appendix has taken up more pages than I intended. I hope at least some of the readers will have followed me up to this point, but it's time to stop, lest I find myself trapped in an ivory tower of my own making.

As far as I know, no other English book has explored nà yīn elements this far, and for that matter very few Chinese books have. Perhaps I can make some pioneering claims, but then they say pioneers are the ones often buried in unmarked graves. It's the settlers on their trail who do well. Let there be many more settlers that come this way ☺

# About the Author

## About the Author
### Hung Hin Cheong (孔憲章)

Hung Hin Cheong (孔憲章) was born in 1946 in Kuala Lumpur, Malaysia. He received his early education in Malaysia before continuing with his tertiary education in the United Kingdom. He graduated with a Bachelor of Science degree with honours (1st class) in electrical and electronic engineering from the University of Leeds, England, in 1969.

He built his career in the electrical industry, and held the position of Chief Executive at a large international electrical equipment manufacturer, before his retirement in 2001.

fēngshuǐ has been the author's passion for many years. He studied under several masters over the years, and was appointed an instructor with the Mastery Academy of Chinese Metaphysics founded by Master Joey Yap, teaching fēngshuǐ and date selection since 2006.

The author was privileged to be schooled in both English and Chinese from a young age. This provided him access to a wide spectrum of fēngshuǐ material available in Chinese, which he perused avidly, ranging from ancient classics to on-line forums. This, together with his upbringing in a family steeped in Chinese traditions, afforded him a rare insight into the cultural background from which fēngshuǐ sprouted. This advantage and his bilingual competence put him in good stead to help propagate classical fēngshuǐ knowledge to the wider world.

## About the Author

The author's engineering training also enabled him to put abstract and often ambigious metaphysical concepts into a structured, logical and practical framework. His papers published in the electronic medium and his earlier books demonstrated his skill in translating and explaining classical texts clearly and succinctly in his own inimitable style. They also showed he was never shy of speaking his own mind when certain old ideas were clearly inconsistent with modern realities.

He has written 4 books on xuán kōng fēngshuǐ, all of which are published by JY Books. These have been very well received by the English speaking fēngshuǐ community.

This new book is a departure from the old pattern in that it deals with sān hè fēngshuǐ, which is as different from xuán kōng as chalk and cheese. It is testament to the author's broad knowledge base and versatility in applying different fēngshuǐ techniques to different tasks.

# JOEY YAP'S
# QI MEN DUN JIA
## Reference Series

**Qi Men Dun Jia**
Compendium
Second edition

**Qi Men Dun Jia**
540 Yang
Structure

**Qi Men Dun Jia**
540 Yin
Structure

**Qi Men Dun Jia**
Year Charts

**Qi Men Dun Jia**
Month Charts

**Qi Men Dun Jia**
Day Charts

**Qi Men Dun Jia**
Day Charts
(San Yuan Method)

**Qi Men Dun Jia**
Forecasting
Method
(Book 1)

**Qi Men Dun Jia**
Forecasting
Method
(Book 2)

**Qi Men Dun Jia**
Evidential
Occurrences

**Qi Men Dun Jia**
Destiny
Analysis

**Qi Men Dun Jia**
Feng Shui

**Qi Men Dun Jia**
Date, Time &
Activity Selection

**Qi Men Dun Jia**
Annual Destiny
Analysis

**Qi Men Dun Jia**
Strategic
Executions

**Qi Men Dun Jia**
The 100
Formations

**Qi Men Dun Jia**
Sun Tzu
Warcraft

**Qi Men Dun Jia**
28 Constellations

**Qi Men Dun Jia**
The Deities

**Qi Men Dun Jia**
The Stars

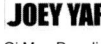
**Qi Men Dun Jia**
The Doors

**Qi Men Dun Jia**
The Stems

This is the most comprehensive reference series to Qi Men Dun Jia in the Chinese Metaphysics world. Exhaustively written for the purpose of facilitating studies and further research, this collection of reference texts and educational books aims to bridge the gap for students who want to learn, and the teachers who want to teach Qi Men.

These essential references provide practical guidance for all branches under the Qi Men Dun Jia studies including Destiny Analysis, Feng Shui, Strategic Executions and Forecasting method.

**These books are available exclusively at:**
**store.joeyyap.com**

Email: order@masteryacademy.com | +6(03) - 2284 8080

# JOEY YAP'S
# QI MEN DUN JIA MASTERY PROGRAM

This is the world's most comprehensive training program on the subject of Qi Men Dun Jia. Joey Yap is the Qi Men Strategist for some of Asia's wealthiest tycoons. This program is modelled after Joey Yap's personal application methods, covering techniques and strategies he applies for his high net worth clients. There is a huge difference between studying the subject as a scholar and learning how to use it successfully as a Qi Men strategist. In this program, Joey Yap shares with you what he personally uses to transform his own life and the lives of million others. In other words, he shares with his students what actually works and not just what looks good in theory with no real practical value. This means that the program covers his personal trade secrets in using the art of Qi Men Dun Jia.

There are five unique programs, with each of them covering one specific application aspect of the Joey Yap's Qi Men Dun Jia system.

Joey Yap's training program focuses on getting results. Theories and formulas are provided in the course workbook so that valuable class time are not wasted dwelling on formulas. Each course comes with its own comprehensive 400-plus pages workbook. Taught once a year exclusively by Joey Yap, seats to these programs are extremely limited.

Getting Whatever You Want from Whatever You've Got™ Spiritual Qi Men™

Qi Men Forecasting Methods™

Qi Men Destiny & Life Transformation™

Qi Men Feng Shui™

Qi Men Strategic Execution™

Qi Men Warcraft™

Call +6(03) 2284 8080 or
email courses@masteryacademy.com for enquiries

www.masteryacademy.com  |  +6(03) - 2284 8080

# JOEY YAP CONSULTING GROUP

## Pioneering Metaphysics-Centric Personal and Corporate Consultations

Founded in 2002, the Joey Yap Consulting Group is the pioneer in the provision of metaphysics-driven coaching and consultation services for professionals and individuals alike. Under the leadership of the renowned international Chinese Metaphysics consultant, author and trainer, Dato' Joey Yap, it has become a world-class specialised metaphysics consulting firm with a strong presence in four continents, meeting the metaphysics-centric needs of its A-list clientele, ranging from celebrities to multinational corporations.

The Group's core consultation practice areas include Feng Shui, BaZi and Qi Men Dun Jia, which are complemented by ancillary services such as Date Selection, Face Reading and Yi Jing. Its team of highly trained professional consultants, led by its Chief Consultant, Dato' Joey Yap, is well-equipped with unparalleled knowledge and experience to help clients achieve their ultimate potentials in various fields and specialisations. Given its credentials, the Group is certainly the firm of choice across the globe for metaphysics-related consultations.

## The Peerless Industry Expert

Benchmarked against the standards of top international consulting firms, our consultants work closely with our clients to achieve the best possible outcomes. The possibilities are infinite as our expertise extends from consultations related to the forces of nature under the subject of Feng Shui, to those related to Destiny Analysis and effective strategising under BaZi and Qi Men Dun Jia respectively.

To date, we have consulted a great diversity of clients, ranging from corporate clients – from various industries such as real estate, finance and telecommunication, amongst others – to the hundreds of thousands of individuals in their key life aspects. Adopting up-to-date and pragmatic approaches, we provide comprehensive services while upholding the importance of clients' priorities and effective outcomes. Recognised as the epitome of Chinese Metaphysics, we possess significant testimonies from worldwide clients as a trusted Brand.

www.joeyyap.com | +6(03) - 2284 8080

## Feng Shui Consultation

**Residential Properties**
- Initial Land/Property Assessment
- Residential Feng Shui Consultation
- Residential Land Selection
- End-to-End Residential Consultation

**Commercial Properties**
- Initial Land/Property Assessment
- Commercial Feng Shui Consultation
- Commercial Land Selection
- End-to-End Commercial Consultation

**Property Developers**
- End-to-End Consultation
- Post-Consultation Advisory Services
- Panel Feng Shui Consultant

**Property Investors**
- Your Personal Feng Shui Consultant
- Tailor-Made Packages

**Memorial Parks & Burial Sites**
- Yin House Feng Shui

## BaZi Consultation

**Personal Destiny Analysis**
- Individual BaZi Analysis
- BaZi Analysis for Families

**Strategic Analysis for Corporate Organizations**
- BaZi Consultations for Corporations
- BaZi Analysis for Human Resource Management

**Entrepreneurs and Business Owners**
- BaZi Analysis for Entrepreneurs

**Career Pursuits**
- BaZi Career Analysis

**Relationships**
- Marriage and Compatibility Analysis
- Partnership Analysis

**General Public**
- Annual BaZi Forecast
- Your Personal BaZi Coach

## Date Selection Consultation

- Marriage Date Selection
- Caesarean Birth Date Selection
- House-Moving Date Selection
- Renovation and Groundbreaking Dates
- Signing of Contracts
- Official Openings
- Product Launches

## Qi Men Dun Jia Consultation

**Strategic Execution**
- Business and Investment Prospects

**Forecasting**
- Wealth and Life Pursuits
- People and Environmental Matters

**Feng Shui**
- Residential Properties
- Commercial Properties

## Speaking Engagement

Many reputable organisations and institutions have worked closely with Joey Yap Consulting Group to build a synergistic business relationship by engaging our team of consultants, which are led by Joey Yap, as speakers at their corporate events.

We tailor our seminars and talks to suit the anticipated or pertinent group of audience. Be it department subsidiary, your clients or even the entire corporation, we aim to fit your requirements in delivering the intended message(s) across.

www.joeyyap.com | +6(03) - 2284 8080

# CHINESE METAPHYSICS REFERENCE SERIES

**The Chinese Metaphysics Reference Series** is a collection of reference texts, source material, and educational textbooks to be used as supplementary guides by scholars, students, researchers, teachers and practitioners of Chinese Metaphysics.

These comprehensive and structured books provide fast, easy reference to aid in the study and practice of various Chinese Metaphysics subjects including Feng Shui, BaZi, Yi Jing, Zi Wei, Liu Ren, Ze Ri, Ta Yi, Qi Men Dun Jia and Mian Xiang.

## The Chinese Metaphysics Compendium

At over 1,000 pages, the Chinese Metaphysics Compendium is a unique one-volume reference book that compiles ALL the formulas relating to Feng Shui, BaZi (Four Pillars of Destiny), Zi Wei (Purple Star Astrology), Yi Jing (I-Ching), Qi Men (Mystical Doorways), Ze Ri (Date Selection), Mian Xiang (Face Reading) and other sources of Chinese Metaphysics.

It is presented in the form of easy-to-read tables, diagrams and reference charts, all of which are compiled into one handy book. This first-of-its-kind compendium is presented in both English and its original Chinese language, so that none of the meanings and contexts of the technical terminologies are lost.

The only essential and comprehensive reference on Chinese Metaphysics, and an absolute must-have for all students, scholars, and practitioners of Chinese Metaphysics.

|  |  |  |  |  |  |  |
|---|---|---|---|---|---|---|
| The Ten Thousand Year Calendar (Pocket Edition) | The Ten Thousand Year Calendar | Dong Gong Date Selection | The Date Selection Compendium | Plum Blossoms Divination Reference Book | Xuan Kong Da Gua Ten Thousand Year Calendar | San Yuan Dragon Gate Eight Formations Water Method |

|  |  |  |  |  |  |  |
|---|---|---|---|---|---|---|
| BaZi Hour Pillar Useful Gods - Wood | BaZi Hour Pillar Useful Gods - Fire | BaZi Hour Pillar Useful Gods - Earth | BaZi Hour Pillar Useful Gods - Metal | BaZi Hour Pillar Useful Gods - Water | Xuan Kong Da Gua Structures Reference Book | Xuan Kong Da Gua 64 Gua Transformation Analysis |

|  |  |  |  |  |  |  |
|---|---|---|---|---|---|---|
| BaZi Structures and Structural Useful Gods - Wood | BaZi Structures and Structural Useful Gods - Fire | BaZi Structures and Structural Useful Gods - Earth | BaZi Structures and Structural Useful Gods - Metal | BaZi Structures and Structural Useful Gods - Water | Earth Study Discern Truth Second Edition | Eight Mansions Bright Mirror |

|  |  |  |  |  |  |  |
|---|---|---|---|---|---|---|
| Secret of Xuan Kong | Ode to Flying Stars | Xuan Kong Purple White Script | Ode to Mysticism | The Yin House Handbook | Water Water Everywhere | Xuan Kong Da Gua Not Exactly For Dummies |

www.masteryacademy.com | +6(03) - 2284 8080

# SAN YUAN QI MEN XUAN KONG DA GUA
## Reference Series

San Yuan Qi Men Xuan Kong Da Gua Compendium

San Yuan Qi Men Xuan Kong Da Gua 540 Yang Structure

San Yuan Qi Men Xuan Kong Da Gua 540 Yin Structure

Xuan Kong Flying Star Secrets Of The 81 Combinations

Xuan Kong Da Gua Fixed Yao Method

Xuan Kong Da Gua Flying Yao Method

Xuan Kong Da Gua 6 Relationships Method

Xuan Kong Flying Star Purple White Script's Advanced Star Charts

The **San Yuan Qi Men Xuan Kong Da Gua Series** is written for the advanced learners in mind. Unlock the secrets to this highly exclusive art and seamlessly integrate both Qi Men Dun Jia and the Xuan Kong Da Gua 64 Hexagrams into one unified practice for effective applications.

This collection is an excellent companion for genuine enthusiasts, students and professional practitioners of the San Yuan Qi Men Xuan Kong Da Gua studies.

## Xuan Kong Collection

### Xuan Kong Flying Stars

This book is an essential introductory book to the subject of Xuan Kong Fei Xing, a well-known and popular system of Feng Shui. Learn 'tricks of the trade' and 'trade secrets' to enhance and maximise Qi in your home or office.

### Xuan Kong Nine Life Star Series (Available in English & Chinese versions)

Joey Yap's Feng Shui Essentials - The Xuan Kong Nine Life Star Series of books comprises of nine individual titles that provide detailed information about each individual Life Star.

Based on the complex and highly-evolved Xuan Kong Feng Shui system, each book focuses on a particular Life Star and provides you with a detailed Feng Shui guide.

www.masteryacademy.com | +6(03) - 2284 8080

# Joey Yap's BaZi Profiling System

## Three Levels of BaZi Profiling (English & Chinese versions)

In BaZi Profiling, there are three levels that reflect three different stages of a person's personal nature and character structure.

### Level 1 – The Day Master

The Day Master in a nutshell is the basic you. The inborn personality. It is your essential character. It answers the basic question "who am I". There are ten basic personality profiles – the ten Day Masters – each with its unique set of personality traits, likes and dislikes.

### Level 2 – The Structure

The Structure is your behavior and attitude – in other words, it is about how you use your personality. It expands on the Day Master (Level 1). The structure reveals your natural tendencies in life – are you a controller, creator, supporter, thinker or connector? Each of the Ten Day Masters express themselves differently through the five Structures. Why do we do the things we do? Why do we like the things we like? The answers are in our BaZi Structure.

### Level 3 – The Profile

The Profile depicts your role in your life. There are ten roles (Ten BaZi Profiles) related to us. As to each to his or her own - the roles we play are different from one another and it is unique to each Profile.

What success means to you, for instance, differs from your friends – this is similar to your sense of achievement or whatever you think of your purpose in life is.

Through the BaZi Profile, you will learn the deeper level of your personality. It helps you become aware of your personal strengths and works as a trigger for you to make all the positive changes to be a better version of you.

Keep in mind, only through awareness that you will be able to maximise your natural talents, abilities and skills. Only then, ultimately, you will get to enter into what we refer as 'flow' of life – a state where you have the powerful force to naturally succeed in life.

**www.BaZiprofiling.com**

# THE BaZi 60 PILLARS SERIES

The BaZi 60 Pillars Series is a collection of ten volumes focusing on each of the Pillars or Jia Zi in BaZi Astrology. Learn how to see BaZi Chart in a new light through the Pictorial Method of BaZi analysis and elevate your proficiency in BaZi studies through this new understanding. Joey Yap's 60 Pillars Life Analysis Method is a refined and enhanced technique that is based on the fundamentals set by the true masters of olden times, and modified to fit to the sophistication of current times.

## BaZi Collection

With these books, leading Chinese Astrology Master Trainer Joey Yap makes it easy to learn how to unlock your Destiny through your BaZi. BaZi or Four Pillars of Destiny is an ancient Chinese science which enables individuals to understand their personality, hidden talents and abilities, as well as their luck cycle - by examining the information contained within their birth data.

Understand and learn more about this accurate ancient science with this BaZi Collection.

BOOK 1

BOOK 2

BOOK 3

BOOK 4

BOOK 5

The 10 Gods

(Available in English & Chinese)

www.masteryacademy.com  |  +6(03) - 2284 8080

# Feng Shui Collection

## Design Your Legacy

Design Your Legacy is Joey Yap's first book on the profound subject of Yin House Feng Shui, which is the study Feng Shui for burials and tombs. Although it is still pretty much a hidden practice that is largely unexplored by modern literature, the significance of Yin House Feng Shui has permeated through the centuries – from the creation of the imperial lineage of emperors in ancient times to the iconic leaders who founded modern China.

This book unveils the true essence of Yin House Feng Shui with its significant applications that are unlike the myths and superstition which have for years, overshadowed the genuine practice itself. Discover how Yin House Feng Shui – the true precursor to all modern Feng Shui practice, can be used to safeguard the future of your descendants and create a lasting legacy.

## Must-Haves for Property Analysis!

For homeowners, those looking to build their own home or even investors who are looking to apply Feng Shui to their homes, these series of books provides valuable information from the classical Feng Shui therioes and applications.

In his trademark straight-to-the-point manner, Joey shares with you the Feng Shui do's and dont's when it comes to finding a property with favorable Feng Shui, which is condusive for home living.

## Stories and Lessons on Feng Shui Series

All in all, this series is a delightful chronicle of Joey's articles, thoughts and vast experience - as a professional Feng Shui consultant and instructor - that have been purposely refined, edited and expanded upon to make for a light-hearted, interesting yet educational read. And with Feng Shui, BaZi, Mian Xiang and Yi Jing all thrown into this one dish, there's something for everyone.

(Available in English & Chinese)

## More Titles under Joey Yap Books

### Pure Feng Shui

Pure Feng Shui is Joey Yap's debut with an international publisher, CICO Books. It is a refreshing and elegant look at the intricacies of Classical Feng Shui - now compiled in a useful manner for modern day readers. This book is a comprehensive introduction to all the important precepts and techniques of Feng Shui practices.

### Your Aquarium Here

This book is the first in Fengshuilogy Series, which is a series of matter-of-fact and useful Feng Shui books designed for the person who wants to do a fuss-free Feng Shui.

# More Titles under Joey Yap Books

### Walking the Dragons

Compiled in one book for the first time from Joey Yap's Feng Shui Mastery Excursion Series, the book highlights China's extensive, vibrant history with astute observations on the Feng Shui of important sites and places. Learn the landform formations of Yin Houses (tombs and burial places), as well as mountains, temples, castles and villages.

### Walking the Dragons : Taiwan Excursion

A Guide to Classical Landform Feng Shui of Taiwan

From China to Tibet, Joey Yap turns his analytical eye towards Taiwan in this extensive Walking the Dragons series. Combined with beautiful images and detailed information about an island once known as Formosa, or "Beautiful Island" in Portuguese, this compelling series of essays highlights the colourful history and wonders of Taiwan. It also provides readers with fascinating insights into the living science of Feng Shui.

### The Art of Date Selection: Personal Date Selection (Available in English & Chinese)

With the Art of Date Selection: Personal Date Selection, you can learn simple, practical methods to select not just good dates, but personalised good dates as well. Whether it is a personal activity such as a marriage or professional endeavour, such as launching a business - signing a contract or even acquiring assets, this book will show you how to pick the good dates and tailor them to suit the activity in question, and to avoid the negative ones too!

### Your Head Here

Your Head Here is the first book by Sherwin Ng. She is an accomplished student of Joey Yap, and an experienced Feng Shui consultant and instructor with Joey Yap Consulting Group and Mastery Academy respectively. It is the second book under the Fengshuilogy series, which focuses on Bedroom Feng Shui, a specific topic dedicated to optimum bed location and placement.

### If the Shoe Fits

This book is for those who want to make the effort to enhance their relationship.

In her debut release, Jessie Lee humbly shares with you the classical BaZi method of the Ten Day Masters and the combination of a new profiling system developed by Joey Yap, to understand and deal with the people around you.

### Being Happy and Successful at Work and in your Career

Have you ever wondered why some of us are so successful in our careers while others are dragging their feet to work or switching from one job to another? Janet Yung hopes to answer this question by helping others through the knowledge and application of BaZi and Chinese Astrology. In her debut release, she shares with the readers the right way of using BaZi to understand themselves: their inborn talents, motivations, skills, and passions, to find their own place in the path of professional development.

### Being Happy & Successful - Managing Yourself & Others

Manage Your Talent & Have Effective Relationships at the Workplace

While many strive for efficiency in the workplace, it is vital to know how to utilize your talents. In this book, Janet Yung will take you further on how to use the BaZi profiling system as a tool to assess your personality and understanding your approach to the job. From ways in communicating with your colleagues to understanding your boss, you will be astounded by what this ancient system can reveal about you and the people in your life. Tips and guidance will also be given in this book so that you will make better decisions for your next step in advancing in your career.

# Face Reading Collection

### The Chinese Art of Face Reading: The Book of Moles

The Book of Moles by Joey Yap delves into the inner meanings of moles and what they reveal about the personality and destiny of an individual. Complemented by fascinating illustrations and Joey Yap's easy-to-understand commentaries and guides, this book takes a deeper focus into a Face Reading subject, which can be used for everyday decisions – from personal relationships to professional dealings and many others.

### Discover Face Reading (Available in English & Chinese)

This is a comprehensive book on all areas of Face Reading, covering some of the most important facial features, including the forehead, mouth, ears and even philtrum above your lips. This book will help you analyse not just your Destiny but also help you achieve your full potential and achieve life fulfillment.

### Joey Yap's Art of Face Reading

The Art of Face Reading is Joey Yap's second effort with CICO Books, and it takes a lighter, more practical approach to Face Reading. This book does not focus on the individual features as it does on reading the entire face. It is about identifying common personality types and characters.

### Faces of Fortune: The 20 Tycoons to bet on over the next 10 years

Faces of Fortune is Tee Lin Say's first book on the subject of Mian Xiang or Chinese Face Reading. As an accomplished Face Reading student of Joey Yap and an experienced business journalist, Lin Say merged both her knowledge into this volume, profiling twenty prominent tycoons in Asia based on the Art of Face Reading.

### Easy Guide on Face Reading (Available in English & Chinese)

The Face Reading Essentials series of books comprises of five individual books on the key features of the face – the Eyes, the Eyebrows, the Ears, the Nose, and the Mouth. Each book provides a detailed illustration and a simple yet descriptive explanation on the individual types of the features.

The books are equally useful and effective for beginners, enthusiasts and those who are curious. The series is designed to enable people who are new to Face Reading to make the most out of first impressions and learn to apply Face Reading skills to understand the personality and character of their friends, family, co-workers and business associates.

## 2018 Annual Releases

| Chinese Astrology for 2018 | Feng Shui for 2018 | Tong Shu Desktop Calendar 2018 | Qi Men Desktop Calendar 2018 | Professional Tong Shu Diary 2018 | Tong Shu Monthly Planner 2018 | Weekly Tong Shu Diary 2018 |

# Cultural Series

## Discover the True Significance of the Ancient Art of Lion Dance

The Lion has long been a symbol of power and strength. That powerful symbol has evolved into an incredible display of a mixture of martial arts and ritualism that is the Lion Dance. Throughout ancient and modern times, the Lion Dance has stamped itself as a popular part of culture, but is there a meaning lost behind this magnificent spectacle?

The Art of Lion Dance written by the world's number one man in Chinese Metaphysics, Dato' Joey Yap, explains the history and origins of the art and its connection to Qi Men Dun Jia. By creating that bridge with Qi Men, the Lion Dance is able to ritualise any type of ceremony, celebrations and mourning alike.

The book is the perfect companion to the modern interpretation of the art as it reveals the significance behind each part of the Lion costume, as well as rituals that are put in place to bring the costume and its spectacle to life.

# Educational Tools and Software

## Joey Yap's Feng Shui Template Set

Directions are the cornerstone of any successful Feng Shui audit or application. The Joey Yap Feng Shui Template Set is a set of three templates to simplify the process of taking directions and determining locations and positions, whether it is for a building, a house, or an open area such as a plot of land - all of it done with just a floor plan or area map.

The Set comprises three basic templates: The Basic Feng Shui Template, Eight Mansions Feng Shui Template, and the Flying Stars Feng Shui Template.

## Mini Feng Shui Compass

The Mini Feng Shui Compass is a self-aligning compass that is not only light at 100gms but also built sturdily to ensure it will be convenient to use anywhere. The rings on the Mini Feng Shui Compass are bilingual and incorporate the 24 Mountain Rings that is used in your traditional Luo Pan.

The comprehensive booklet included with this, will guide you in applying the 24 Mountain Directions on your Mini Feng Shui Compass effectively and the Eight Mansions Feng Shui to locate the most auspicious locations within your home, office and surroundings. You can also use the Mini Feng Shui Compass when measuring the direction of your property for the purpose of applying Flying Stars Feng Shui.

www.masteryacademy.com | +6(03) - 2284 8080

# MASTERY ACADEMY
## OF CHINESE METAPHYSICS
Your **Preferred** Choice to the Art & Science of Classical Chinese Metaphysics Studies

Bringing **innovative** techniques and **creative** teaching methods to an ancient study.

**Mastery Academy of Chinese Metaphysics** was established by Joey Yap to play the role of disseminating this Eastern knowledge to the modern world with the belief that this valuable knowledge should be accessible to everyone and everywhere.

Its goal is to enrich people's lives through accurate, professional teaching and practice of Chinese Metaphysics knowledge globally. It is the first academic institution of its kind in the world to adopt the tradition of Western institutions of higher learning - where students are encouraged to explore, question and challenge themselves, as well as to respect different fields and branches of studies. This is done together with the appreciation and respect of classical ideas and applications that have stood the test of time.

The Art and Science of Chinese Metaphysics — be it Feng Shui, BaZi (Astrology), Qi Men Dun Jia, Mian Xiang (Face Reading), ZeRi (Date Selection) or Yi Jing — is no longer a field shrouded with mystery and superstition. In light of new technology, fresher interpretations and innovative methods, as well as modern teaching tools like the Internet, interactive learning, e-learning and distance learning, anyone from virtually any corner of the globe, who is keen to master these disciplines can do so with ease and confidence under the guidance and support of the Academy.

It has indeed proven to be a centre of educational excellence for thousands of students from over thirty countries across the world; many of whom have moved on to practice classical Chinese Metaphysics professionally in their home countries.

At the Academy, we believe in enriching people's lives by empowering their destinies through the disciplines of Chinese Metaphysics. Learning is not an option - it is a way of life!

MASTERY ACADEMY
OF CHINESE METAPHYSICS™

**MALAYSIA**
19-3, The Boulevard, Mid Valley City, 59200 Kuala Lumpur, Malaysia
Tel : +6(03)-2284 8080 | Fax : +6(03)-2284 1218
Email      : info@masteryacademy.com
Website  : www.masteryacademy.com

---

Australia, Austria, Canada, China, Croatia, Cyprus, Czech Republic, Denmark, France, Germany, Greece, Hungary, India, Italy, Kazakhstan, Malaysia, Netherlands (Holland), New Zealand, Philippines, Poland, Russian Federation, Singapore, Slovenia, South Africa, Switzerland, Turkey, United States of America, Ukraine, United Kingdom

www.masteryacademy.com | +6(03) - 2284 8080

## BaZi 10X

Emphasising on the practical aspects of BaZi, this programme is rich with numerous applications and techniques pertaining to the pursuit of wealth, health, relationship and career, all of which constitute the formula of success. This programme is designed for all levels of practitioners and is supplemented with innovative learning materials to enable easy learning. Discover the different layers of BaZi from a brand new perspective with BaZi 10X.

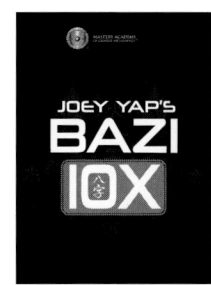

## Feng Shui for Life

This is an entry-level five-day course designed for the Feng Shui beginner to learn the application of practical Feng Shui in day-to-day living. Lessons include quick tips on analysing the BaZi chart, simple Feng Shui solutions for the home, basic Date Selection, useful Face Reading techniques and practical Water formulas. A great introduction course on Chinese Metaphysics studies for beginners.

## Joey Yap's Design Your Destiny

This is a three-day life transformation program designed to inspire awareness and action for you to create a better quality of life. It introduces the DRT™ (Decision Referential Technology) method, which utilises the BaZi Personality Profiling system to determine the right version of you, and serves as a tool to help you make better decisions and achieve a better life in the least resistant way possible, based on your Personality Profile Type.

# Mian Xiang Mastery™
## LIVE COURSES (MODULES ONE AND TWO)

This program comprises of two modules, each carefully developed to allow students to familiarise with the fundamentals of Mian Xiang or Face Reading and the intricacies of its theories and principles. With lessons guided by video lectures, presentations and notes, students are able to understand and practice Mian Xiang with greater depth.

**Module One:** Basic Face Reading

**Module Two:** Practical Face Reading

# Yi Jing Mastery™
## LIVE COURSES (MODULES ONE AND TWO)

Whether you are a casual or serious Yi Jing enthusiast, this lesson-based program contains two modules that brings students deeper into the Chinese science of divination. The lessons will guide students on the mastery of its sophisticated formulas and calculations to derive answers to questions we pose.

**Module One:** Traditional Yi Jing

**Module Two:** Plum Blossom Numerology

# Ze Ri Mastery™
## LIVE COURSES (MODULES ONE AND TWO)

In two modules, students will undergo a thorough instruction on the fundamentals of ZeRi or Date Selection. The comprehensive program covers Date Selection for both Personal and Feng Shui purposes to Xuan Kong Da Gua Date Selection.

**Module One:** Personal and Feng Shui Date Selection

**Module Two:** Xuan Kong Da Gua Date Selection

# Joey Yap's
## San Yuan Qi Men Xuan Kong Da Gua™

This is an advanced level program which can be summed up as the Integral Vision of San Yuan studies – an integration of the ancient potent discipline of Qi Men Dun Jia and the highly popular Xuan Kong 64 Hexagrams. Often regarded as two independent systems, San Yuan Qi Men and San Yuan Xuan Kong Da Gua can trace their origins to the same source and were actually used together in ancient times by great Chinese sages.

This method enables practitioners to harness the Qi of time and space, and predict the outcomes through a highly-detailed analysis of landforms, places and sites.

www.masteryacademy.com | +6(03) - 2284 8080

## Feng Shui Mastery™
### LIVE COURSES (MODULES ONE TO FOUR)

This an ideal program for those who wants to achieve mastery in Feng Shui from the comfort of their homes. This comprehensive program covers the foundation up to the advanced practitioner levels, touching upon the important theories from various classical Feng Shui systems including Ba Zhai, San Yuan, San He and Xuan Kong.

**Module One:** Beginners Course  
**Module Two:** Practitioners Course  
**Module Three:** Advanced Practitioners Course  
**Module Four:** Master Course

## BaZi Mastery™
### LIVE COURSES (MODULES ONE TO FOUR)

This lesson-based program brings a thorough introduction to BaZi and guides the student step-by-step, all the way to the professional practitioner level. From the theories to the practical, BaZi students along with serious Feng Shui practitioners, can master its application with accuracy and confidence.

**Module One:** Intensive Foundation Course  
**Module Two:** Practitioners Course  
**Module Three:** Advanced Practitioners Course  
**Module Four:** Master Course in BaZi

## Xuan Kong Mastery™
### LIVE COURSES (MODULES ONE TO THREE)
*\* Advanced Courses For Master Practitioners*

Xuan Kong is a sophisticated branch of Feng Shui, replete with many techniques and formulae, which encompass numerology, symbology and the science of the Ba Gua, along with the mathematics of time. This program is ideal for practitioners looking to bring their practice to a more in-depth level.

**Module One:** Advanced Foundation Course  
**Module Two A:** Advanced Xuan Kong Methodologies  
**Module Two B:** Purple White  
**Module Three:** Advanced Xuan Kong Da Gua

www.masteryacademy.com | +6(03) - 2284 8080

# The Mastery Academy around the world!

www.masteryacademy.com | +6(03) - 2284 8080

## Millionaire Feng Shui Secrets Programme

This program is geared towards maximising your financial goals and dreams through the use of Feng Shui. Focusing mainly on the execution of Wealth Feng Shui techniques such as Luo Shu sectors and more, it is perfect for boosting careers, businesses and investment opportunities.

## Grow Rich With BaZi Programme

This comprehensive programme covers the foundation of BaZi studies and presents information from the career, wealth and business standpoint. This course is ideal for those who want to maximise their wealth potential and live the life they deserve. Knowledge gained in this course will be used as driving factors to encourage personal development towards a better future.

## Walk the Mountains!
## Learn Feng Shui in a Practical and Hands-on Program

 ### Feng Shui Mastery Excursion™

Learn landform (Luan Tou) Feng Shui by walking the mountains and chasing the Dragon's vein in China. This program takes the students in a study tour to examine notable Feng Shui landmarks, mountains, hills, valleys, ancient palaces, famous mansions, houses and tombs in China. The excursion is a practical hands-on course where students are shown to perform readings using the formulas they have learnt and to recognise and read Feng Shui Landform (Luan Tou) formations.

Read about the China Excursion here:
http://www.fengshuiexcursion.com

---

Mastery Academy courses are conducted around the world. Find out when will Joey Yap be in your area by visiting
**www.masteryacademy.com**
or call our offices at **+6(03)-2284 8080**.

# Online Home Study Courses

Gain Valuable Knowledge from the Comfort of Your Home

Now, armed with your trusty computer or laptop and Internet access, the knowledge of Chinese Metaphysics is just a click away!

## 3 Easy Steps to Activate Your Home Study Course:

### Step 1:
Go to the URL as indicated on the Activation Card and key in your Activation Code

### Step 2:
At the Registration page, fill in the details accordingly to enable us to generate your Student Identification (Student ID).

### Step 3:
Upon successful registration, you may begin your lessons immediately.

## Joey Yap's Feng Shui Mastery HomeStudy Course

Module 1: **Empowering Your Home**
Module 2: **Master Practitioner Program**
Learn how easy it is to harness the power of the environment to promote health, wealth and prosperity in your life. The knowledge and applications of Feng Shui will not be a mystery but a valuable tool you can master on your own.

## Joey Yap's BaZi Mastery HomeStudy Course

Module 1: **Mapping Your Life**
Module 2: **Mastering Your Future**
Discover your path of least resistance to success with insights about your personality and capabilities, and what strengths you can tap on to maximise your potential for success and happiness by mastering BaZi (Chinese Astrology). This course will teach you all the essentials you need to interpret a BaZi chart and more.

## Joey Yap's Mian Xiang Mastery HomeStudy Course

Module 1: **Face Reading**
Module 2: **Advanced Face Reading**
A face can reveal so much about a person. Now, you can learn the Art and Science of Mian Xiang (Chinese Face Reading) to understand a person's character based on his or her facial features, with ease and confidence.